Raising Warriors: Nurturing Boys to be Emotionally Intelligent & Mentally Strong.

This is a parents' easy guide to helping young boys succeed in all areas of their lives by mastering their emotions, building grit, and cultivating a growth mindset.

Kaye Buenaventure

To my beloved Axl Mateo,

You are the inspiration behind every word in this book. Your boundless curiosity, strength, and kindness have shown me the incredible potential within every boy. Your journey is my greatest joy, and your growth is my proudest achievement.

Contents

Introduction

One chilly autumn evening, a young boy named Jacob stood on the sidelines of his soccer game, his eyes fixed on the ground. Just moments before, a missed goal had sent a wave of frustration through him, and his reaction—a mix of tears and anger—had been visible for all to see. Fast forward six months, and there's Jacob again, this time with a steady gaze and a calm demeanor, even after a similar misstep. What changed? The transformation began at home, with a new approach to understanding and managing his emotions, a method that reinforced resilience and mental strength.

This book is crafted for anyone who plays a pivotal role in nurturing boys like Jacob. It is a thorough guide designed to empower you, providing the tools and knowledge to cultivate emotional intelligence and mental strength in young boys. These skills are not just about managing emotions or persevering through challenges; they're about thriving in a complex world. I understand that implementing these strategies may not always be easy, but I'm here to support you every step of the way.

What sets this book apart is its blend of customizable emotional intelligence plans, such as the 'Emotion Wheel' and 'Feelings Journal', interactive components like 'Role-Play Scenarios' and 'Group Discussions', and a keen focus on contemporary challenges. Whether you're a parent worried about digital distractions, an educator striving to foster a supportive classroom, or a caregiver navigating the nuances of modern masculinity, this book offers tools and strategies tailored to your needs and those of the boys in your care.

I understand your concerns and aspirations for these young individuals. That's why I've ensured that every piece of advice in this book is rooted in the latest psychological research yet presented practically and free of jargon. From worksheets to different resources and suggestions, each element is designed to provide a hands-on learning experience, making applying these concepts to everyday life seamless and practical.

Moreover, this book doesn't just focus on the individual development of boys but also emphasizes the importance of community. It offers strategies for building supportive networks through schools, sports teams, and online forums, reinforcing that it takes a village to raise a child. By fostering these connections, we can create a supportive environment that nurtures young boys' emotional intelligence and mental strength, making them feel valued and understood.

As someone deeply committed to the emotional well-being and success of young boys, I've poured my passion into these pages, providing you with guidance that is both evidence-based and easy to understand. We will embark on this journey together about transforming the boys in our lives. Your role as a caregiver is crucial in this process. As we learn and grow, we will discover new ways to support and nurture their emotional intelligence and mental strength.

I invite you to join me on this transformative journey. By the time you turn the last page, you will be equipped to nurture not just boys but emotionally intelligent and mentally strong warriors, ready to face the world with confidence and resilience. Let's begin this important work together, for their future—ours—depends on it.

Chapter One

Understanding Emotional Intelligence in Boys

H ave you ever watched a boy navigate a moment of frustration, like struggling with a puzzle or feeling left out at the playground? Moments like these lay the groundwork for learning how to manage emotions and interact with others. Emotional intelligence isn't just a set of skills reserved for adulthood; it begins to form in the earliest years of life. In this chapter, we delve deep into the fabric of emotional intelligence—what it is, why it's so crucial during early development, and how different cultures shape its expression in boys. This isn't just about helping boys manage a temporary tantrum; it's about equipping them with the skills to face life's challenges with confidence and understanding.

1.1 Decoding Emotional Intelligence: Beyond the Basics

Defining Emotional Intelligence

Emotional intelligence is a term that echoes through classrooms, psychology texts, and parenting discussions, often simplified to just recognizing and reacting to one's own emotions and those of others. Yet, it extends beyond emotional awareness; it is also about managing these emotions effectively, empathizing with others, and navigating complex social settings with finesse. Think of it as a toolkit that includes a variety of skills—from understanding why your friend is sad, to resolving a conflict without losing your cool, to staying motivated to finish a task even when it feels daunting.

Importance in Early Development

Emotional intelligence takes root in early childhood, a pivotal period for emotional and social development. Beyond cognitive achievements, these years are crucial for emotional education. As young boys learn to identify and appropriately respond to their emotions, they lay the groundwork for healthier relationships, improved stress management, and enhanced problem-solving abilities. This time is significant for boys, who may face societal pressure to hide their vulnerability, to learn that emotional understanding and regulation are not weaknesses but strengths.

Recognizing Emotional Intelligence

Recognizing emotional intelligence in boys is a subtle yet rewarding journey. It's like observing a seed's growth. Manifestations of emerging emotional intelligence encompass a boy's capacity to articulate his emotions, whether upset or joyful, his initiative to console peers, and his curiosity about others' feelings. These behaviors show his growing ability to navigate emotions, giving us valuable moments to step in and offer guidance and support.

Cultural Perspectives on Emotional Intelligence

Cultural norms significantly influence the development and expression of emotional intelligence. While some cultures prize emotional restraint, discouraging boys from showing vulnerability, others celebrate emotional openness, encouraging boys to express their feelings freely. Recognizing and respecting these cultural differences is essential for tailoring emotional intelligence education effectively. Incorporating activities that allow the sharing of personal experiences and cultural traditions in diverse settings, such as multicultural classrooms, can enhance emotional understanding and respect among boys from varied backgrounds.

Interactive Element: Reflective Journal Prompt

To help you apply these insights, consider keeping a *reflective journal* as you read through this book. Here's a prompt to get you started: Think about a recent interaction with a boy in your care—perhaps a moment of emotional expression or a conflict resolution. How did you respond, and what was the outcome? Reflect on what this interaction might reveal about his stage of emotional intelligence development and consider what strategies you could use to further nurture his emotional skills.

1.2 The Early Signs of Emotional Intelligence in Toddlers

Observing toddlers at play reveals their physical and language growth and the early stages of emotional intelligence. This crucial period sees toddlers beginning to recognize and name emotions in themselves and others, marking the onset of empathy. It's akin to the first signs of growth in a garden, indicating that a flourishing emotional landscape can emerge with proper nurturing. Toddlers might point to smiling faces in books, labeling them "happy," or express sadness verbally when experiencing disappointment. This capacity to link emotions with language lays the groundwork for emotional intelligence. While parenting or teaching, spotting these signs requires attentiveness. Creating an environment that encourages emotional expression allows toddlers to feel secure in showing a range of feelings. When toddlers express emotions, labeling these moments openly, such as acknowledging upset feelings when a toy falls, validates their experience and teaches them to articulate their emotions.

Observing their interactions with peers, like showing concern for a crying friend, indicates developing empathy. Fostering emotional intelligence transcends mere observation; it demands active involvement. Validating feelings, for example, involves more than dismissing their frustrations with a simple "It's okay." Instead, empathizing with their situation, like acknowledging the annoyance of puzzle pieces not fitting, affirms their feelings and encourages emotional understanding.

Challenges in nurturing emotional growth stem from toddlers' limited vocabulary, making it hard for them to fully express complex emotions and their egocentric perspective, which complicates teaching empathy. Simplifying language and regularly naming emotions can help bridge this gap, while shared activities like reading about feelings or sharing toys can foster empathy. Patience is essential, as each toddler develops at their own pace.

Maintaining a supportive environment, using language as an emotional development tool, and modeling desired behaviors will cultivate the seeds of emotional intelligence planted during these early years. With time and consistent effort, these initial signs of emotional intelligence will grow into lifelong skills.

1.3 Nurturing Empathy: The First Step Towards Emotional Intelligence

Empathy, the ability to understand and share another person's feelings, is not just a nice-to-have skill; it's the foundation of emotional intelligence and a critical component of successful interpersonal relationships. Think of empathy as the glue that holds human connections together. This bridge allows individuals to cross over into each other's experiences and view the world from another perspective. For young boys, developing empathy is crucial. It helps them build friendships, collaborate in team settings, and navigate the complex social landscapes they will encounter.

Teaching empathy to boys can be approached in several practical ways. *Storytelling* is one of the most powerful tools at your disposal. Through stories, boys can explore diverse emotions and situations, stepping into characters' shoes from different backgrounds and circumstances. This entertains them and opens their minds to a broader range of human experiences. For instance, when reading a story about a character who faces a dilemma or suffers a loss, pause and discuss how that character might feel with the boy. Ask questions like, **"How would you feel in their place?"** or **"What would you do if you were them?"** This not only stimulates empathy but also enhances critical thinking.

Another key method is *discussing emotions* openly. In everyday life, take moments to discuss how specific actions might make others feel. This could be as simple as talking about how a sibling might feel when one boy shares his toys with them or how a friend might feel when they help them with a difficult task. It's important to highlight positive and negative emotions, as understanding a broad spectrum of feelings strengthens emotional intelligence.

Role-playing is another dynamic approach. It allows boys to act out various scenarios that might evoke different emotions. For example, you could set up a scenario where one boy has taken another's toy without asking. Guide them through expressing how each character might feel and discussing better ways to handle the situation. This active participation engages the learning process and cements understanding as boys explore empathy in real time.

The role of caregivers in this process cannot be overstressed. Children learn a great deal by observing the adults in their lives. When you demonstrate empathy in your actions—perhaps by expressing concern for a neighbour who is unwell or showing understanding to a waiter who mixed up your order—you provide a live example for boys to emulate. Your reactions to everyday situations are powerful lessons in empathy, teaching boys that understanding others' feelings and perspectives is a valuable part of human interaction.

Empathy requires action, like consoling a friend or inviting a solitary classmate to join. It equips boys with skills for strong relationships, leadership, and fulfillment. Emphasizing empathy builds emotional intelligence, which is crucial for their growth. Every discussion, story, and role-play enhances their empathy and emotional intelligence.

1.4 Emotional Regulation Skills for Preschoolers

Understanding emotional regulation in the context of preschoolers is akin to learning how to use the brakes on a bicycle. It's about finding that balance where they can still enjoy the ride but also know how to slow down or stop when necessary. Emotional regulation is crucial in early childhood development as it lays the groundwork for how these young minds will handle their feelings throughout life. It involves recognizing their emotions, understanding how to respond to them appropriately, and managing their intensity and expression in a way that is adapted to their environment. For preschoolers, this could mean learning to *take deep breaths* when upset instead of throwing toys or using words to express frustration instead of resorting to tantrums.

Though challenging, teaching emotional regulation to preschoolers can be effectively managed with the right strategies. An essential technique is deep breathing, a simple yet powerful tool. Transform it into a playful activity by imagining the inflation of a balloon or the scent of a favorite flower to encourage slow, calming breaths. Another effective method involves guiding them to *articulate their feelings*, shifting from expressions of anger to more nuanced statements like, **"I feel upset because I wanted to play with that toy."** This not only defuses tense situations but also deepens their emotional understanding. Equally important is creating a supportive environment characterized by consistency, predictability, and safety.

Children benefit from knowing what comes next, such as the sequence of playtime, snack time, and story time. This predictability aids in emotional management by reducing unforeseen stressors. Additionally, establishing a *safe space* where emotions can be freely expressed—such as a *cozy corner* with soft pillows and calming visuals—encourages open emotional expression without fear of judgment or punishment. This approach fosters a secure environment conducive to learning and emotional growth.

Teaching emotional regulation to preschoolers faces challenges, notably inconsistent discipline. Mixed messages about acceptable emotional expressions can confuse children, leading to more difficulty in managing their emotions. For instance, alternating between scolding and ignoring a child's anger fails to provide clear guidance on appropriate behavior. Consistent responses clarify expected behaviors, simplifying emotional regulation for children. Additionally, caregiver behavior plays a vital role. Children observe and mimic adult reactions to stress; thus, caregivers exhibiting calm and controlled responses in stressful situations model effective emotional regulation. Caregivers must remain aware of their influence, as their behaviors serve as direct learning examples for children.

Addressing these challenges requires patience, consistency, and proactive teaching strategies. It's about equipping preschoolers with the foundational skills for constructive emotional management and fostering a supportive environment for developing emotionally intelligent and resilient individuals.

1.5 Building Emotional Vocabulary in Early Childhood

The importance of a rich emotional vocabulary for young boys cannot be overstated. Equipping them to accurately express and manage their feelings is crucial for their emotional and mental development. This skill facilitates their self-expression and enhances their empathy and social connections. Integrating emotional vocabulary into daily routines is straightforward. *Story time*, for instance, offers a prime opportunity to introduce new emotional words. By discussing characters' feelings and motivations, boys learn to relate these emotions to their own experiences, fostering a deeper understanding of themselves and others. During story time, I try to tell the characters' situations to my son's everyday experiences to immerse him in the characters' emotions.

Another effective tool is *daily check-ins* about emotions. Asking boys to describe their feelings about the day's events encourages them to practice their emotional vocabulary, promoting reflection and learning from daily experiences. Introducing complex emotions requires using age-appropriate language. Begin with fundamental emotions and introduce more nuanced feelings, using visual aids like emotion charts to help boys connect words to emotions.

Consistent practice and positive reinforcement are essential to mastering emotional vocabulary. Engaging in regular conversations about feelings and acknowledging the correct use of emotional words encourages boys to refine their emotional expressions. This not only motivates them but also affirms the validity and importance of their feelings. By incorporating these practices into daily life, boys develop a robust emotional vocabulary, a crucial tool in their emotional intelligence toolbox. This ability will significantly impact their social interactions, resilience, and overall well-being, guiding them through life's challenges and relationships.

1.6 Role-Playing Scenarios to Enhance Emotional Understanding

Role-playing goes beyond simple play as an invaluable tool to foster empathy, perspective-taking, and emotional regulation. Simulating real-life scenarios, such as sharing toys or navigating disagreements, allows boys to understand the emotional consequences of their actions in a supportive environment. It's essential to design role-plays that mirror actual challenges, including peer conflicts or bullying, combining clear guidance with the chance for boys to make their own decisions. This mimics the complexity of real situations. During role-play, minimal intervention from observers is vital, giving boys space to explore their interactions, promoting independence, and enriching their learning experience. A debriefing session following the role-play supports introspection and discussion, further deepening their grasp of emotional dynamics and improving their conflict resolution abilities.

Incorporating feedback into role-playing exercises is about nurturing growth and learning rather than just pointing out what went wrong. Provide specific, constructive, and, most importantly, kind feedback. For instance, if a boy reacted aggressively during a scenario, instead of saying, "Don't do that," you might say, **"I saw that you got really upset when Jason took your ball. Maybe next time, you could tell him why that upset you and ask for it back politely."** It's also beneficial to encourage the boys to give feedback to each other, guiding them to do so respectfully and helpfully. This builds their skills in giving and receiving feedback and enhances their empathy and understanding of each other's emotional states.

Role-playing transforms the abstract concept of emotional intelligence into concrete experiences. By embedding empathy, perspective-taking, and emotional regulation into daily activities, boys can explore and grow in a supportive setting. This practical method teaches them about their emotions and arms them with strategies for effective management. Engaging in these scenarios enhances their understanding of different emotional states and bolsters their ability to self-regulate. Over time, they develop a repertoire of responses that enable them to navigate emotional complexities skillfully, leading to greater emotional maturity.

Interactive Element: Role-play a Problematic Situation

Have you ever witnessed your son being bullied or pushed around in the playground? How did you feel? How did you react? Did his actions make you proud, or did you need to work on this? Try this activity and see how it goes.

Plan a role-playing session for boys in your care. It could be with their peers or siblings or, better yet, parents/caregivers pretending to be kids. Make it fun, but note the responses they will give to different scenarios and be intentional in creating a safe space for them to express their emotions. Then, be prepared for the conversation you need to address.

CHAPTER HIGHLIGHTS & ACTION POINTS:

- Keep a *'reflective journal'* to record any recent interaction with the boy in your care and note their emotional intelligence and development stage, as well as strategies to use in nurturing his emotional skills.

- Observe and Engage:

  - Use these moments to guide and support them in managing their emotions. Watch for moments when boys experience frustration or feel left out.

- Practical ways of teaching empathy to little boys:

  - *Storytelling & Role-playing.* Discuss emotions openly and highlighting both positive and negative feelings.

- Emotional Regulation Strategies

  - Teach deep breathing as a calming technique.. Practice this in a playful way like:

    - Inflating a balloon

    - Imagining smelling the scent of a flower

  - Encourage boys to articulate their feelings with words.

  - Create a predictable and safe environment for emotional expression

  - Avoid inconsistent discipline, i.e., alternating scolding and ignoring a child's anger.

Emotion Wheel Chart

- Expand their emotional vocabulary through:

    ◦ Discussing character's feelings and motivations during storytime

    ◦ Daily check-ins to see how they feel about the day's events.

    ◦ Visuals like *an Emotion wheel chart* to aid in their vocabulary

    ◦ Reinforce the use of emotional language with positive feedback.

Chapter Two

Developing Emotional Intelligence Through Play

I magine a regular afternoon in the park, where children's laughter fills the air. Among them is little Ethan, who, during a game of tag, pauses to help a younger child who has stumbled and fallen. It's not just a moment of kindness; it's a demonstration of emotional intelligence in action, nurtured through play. Play isn't merely a way for children to pass the time; it's the arena where they learn to interact with the world around them. This chapter explores how play can be a structured yet fun way to develop crucial emotional intelligence skills in boys.

2.1 Designing Emotionally Intelligent Playtimes

Transforming playtime into a rich environment for emotional learning means using every game and interaction to nurture empathy, self-regulation, and teamwork. For instance, a game like 'Simon Says' can teach emotional awareness by including commands that encourage emotional expressions, such as "Simon says, show me a happy face." Choosing toys and games that promote emotional education is key. Cooperative board games that highlight teamwork and action figures for role-playing help boys develop the skills to navigate social and emotional challenges in a safe environment. Selecting toys that encourage open-ended play enhances self-expression and emotional discovery.

The balance between structured and unstructured play is also crucial in developing emotional intelligence. Structured play, which includes organized games or activities with specific rules, helps children learn how to follow guidelines, take turns, and manage their emotions during structured interactions. On the other hand, unstructured play, such as free playtime in a sandbox or on a playground, gives children the freedom to make their own decisions, use their imagination, and interact with peers on their own terms. Both forms of play are important, as they provide different opportunities for emotional growth. For example, while playing in a sandbox, a child might decide to share his shovel with another, a small act that demonstrates empathy and sharing, while a structured turn-taking game teaches patience and self-control.

Interactive Element: Playtime Planning Worksheet

To help you integrate these concepts into your daily routine, consider using the 'Playtime Planning Worksheet.' This tool can help you balance structured and unstructured play, choose emotionally enriching toys, and design activities that specifically focus on developing emotional intelligence. It's a practical way to apply the strategies discussed and make playtime a rich source of emotional learning.

Playtime is vital for bonding between caregivers and children, offering a relaxed setting to observe and interact. This interaction fosters trust and understanding, revealing insights into a child's emotional needs and development. Participation in play, like board games or role-playing with action figures, not only reinforces emotional learning but also demonstrates the value placed on the child's experiences. Such moments of trust and enjoyment are fertile ground for emotional intelligence to thrive. Through play, skills such as empathy, self-regulation, and cooperation are not just learned but lived, equipping boys to adeptly navigate their emotions and face life's challenges with emotional intelligence.

2.2 Games That Grow Emotional Intelligence

In the world of parenting and teaching, finding ways to make emotional intelligence learning exciting for boys is like unlocking a treasure chest of possibilities. Board games, those timeless favorites cherished for their fun factor, are actually hidden gems for nurturing emotional skills. Take classics like '**The Game of Life**' or '**Candy Land**'—they're not just about rolling dice and moving pieces; they're mini emotional roller coasters. Playing these games isn't just about winning; it's about learning to handle the highs and lows with grace. And the best part? They spark conversations about feelings and strategies that stick with us long after the game is over.

Now, let's step onto the field or court. Think about a pickup soccer game or a friendly run around the block. These aren't just about scoring goals or beating personal records; they're about managing excitement, frustration, and even exhaustion. They're the playgrounds where boys learn to recognize and tame those roller-coaster emotions. And when they're part of a team, it's not just about winning together; it's about supporting each other through every bump in the road.

And who can forget storytelling? Picture this: huddling around a table with dice in hand, creating worlds and characters with just a roll. Games like '**Rory's Story Cubes**' aren't just about crafting tales; they're about diving deep into emotions and experiences. They're about stepping into someone else's shoes and seeing the world through their eyes. It's like having a front-row seat to the theater of empathy.

Now, let's get creative. Imagine crafting your own game tailored to your boy's emotions. Maybe it's a simple card game where each card represents a different feeling, or perhaps it's a storytelling adventure where every twist and turn teaches a lesson about resilience or empathy. The possibilities are endless, and the journey is as exciting as it is enlightening.

So, whether we're rolling the dice, kicking a ball, or spinning tales, the adventure of growing emotional intelligence through play is a journey worth embarking on. It's not just about winning or losing; it's about discovering the magic of emotions and the power of connection—one game at a time.

2.3 The Role of Sports in Emotional Development

When young boys step onto the playing field, they're not just mastering the game's rules or perfecting their throws; they're entering a classroom teeming with lessons in emotional intelligence. Sportsmanship, a term tossed around in youth sports, boils down to respect, empathy, and self-regulation—pillars of emotional intelligence. Picture a young soccer player shaking hands with the opposing team after a tough loss. That act of sportsmanship isn't just about etiquette; it's gracefully handling disappointment, acknowledging others' efforts, and maintaining respect, even in defeat.

Linking sportsmanship with emotional intelligence starts with realizing that how we behave in sports mirrors how we tackle life's challenges. Through sports, boys learn to handle their emotions when the game doesn't go their way. They grasp empathy by witnessing others' disappointment and offering support. This shared emotional journey teaches them that their actions ripple out, impacting others directly—a lesson critical for broader social skills and emotional awareness.

Selecting the right sports for a boy should be a mix of personal interests and developmental needs. It's crucial to involve him in sports he's genuinely excited about; intrinsic motivation makes learning and participation more natural. However, consider how different sports contribute to emotional growth. Team sports like soccer and basketball foster cooperation and empathy as players unite toward common goals. Individual sports like martial arts promote self-regulation and discipline. Striking a balance ensures engagement while nurturing emotional and social development.

A coach's role extends beyond teaching game skills; they're mentors in emotional intelligence. A coach who discusses players' feelings during games teaches emotional intelligence actively. They model respect and empathy, providing real-life examples for boys to follow on and off the field.

In sports, learning from wins and losses is essential for emotional growth. Discussing post-game highs and lows transforms defeats into valuable lessons. Boys should be encouraged to see setbacks as opportunities for growth. Celebrating effort and progress fosters resilience and a positive approach to challenges, which is vital for personal development.

Sports aren't just about physical health or fun; they're integral to emotional education. They offer a structured yet dynamic setting for boys to learn crucial life skills—handling emotions, teamwork, conflict resolution, and resilience. These lessons, learned in the heat of the game, shape them into emotionally intelligent individuals ready to face life's challenges head-on.

2.4 Creative Arts as a Tool for Emotional Expression

Imagine a boy sitting with his colors, pouring his heart onto a canvas. Each brushstroke tells a story—a silent conversation between him and his emotions. The heaviness of his strokes speaks of anger and sadness, while bright splashes of color whisper of joy and excitement. In his art, he finds a sanctuary—a place where feelings flow freely, understood without words.

Creating art isn't just about making something beautiful; it's about finding confidence and pride in oneself. With every sketch or sculpture, he discovers the magic of his own imagination, building a sense of accomplishment that radiates from within. And when he shares his creations, we embark on a journey together, exploring the depths of his emotions with every stroke and shade.

Now, let's sway to the rhythm of music and dance. With every beat of the drum, he releases pent-up energy, feeling the exhilaration in his bones. His voice becomes a melody—a reflection of his joys and sorrows, sung out for the world to hear. And in the dance, in the graceful movements and spontaneous gestures, he finds freedom—a way to express himself without words.

In the world of drama and theater, he steps into different roles, each one a new adventure in empathy and understanding. As he navigates the stage, he learns to think on his feet, adapting to the twists and turns of the story. With every character he portrays, he gains a deeper insight into the human experience, growing not just as an actor but as a person.

Creating a space for artistic expression at home is simple yet profound. It's about providing the tools, carving out a corner, and most importantly, being present to celebrate every moment of creativity. With each doodle and dance step, we cherish the journey, embracing the messiness of creation and the beauty of self-discovery.

Through art, music, dance, and drama, he explores the depths of his emotions and discovers the richness of the human experience. Guided by our love and encouragement, he learns to navigate the highs and lows with resilience and grace. As he paints, plays, dances, and acts, he not only creates art but also finds himself amidst the colors and melodies of his own emotions.

2.5 Digital Games: Selecting the Right Ones for Emotional Growth

In the whirlwind of digital screens that surround us, guiding our boys through their digital adventures isn't just a task—it's a chance for them to grow emotionally. The right games can do more than just fill their time; they can shape their understanding of teamwork, empathy, and problem-solving. But with countless options at their fingertips, how do we make sure they're playing games that enrich their hearts and minds?

When picking out games that nurture emotional intelligence, keep an eye out for ones that encourage kindness and cooperation. Games where players team up to solve puzzles or help each other through challenges subtly teach the value of working together and understanding others' feelings. Similarly, games that require tough decisions affecting the fates of characters can help boys see the ripple effects of their actions from different perspectives—an essential skill for building empathy.

Problem-solving games are another gem. Opt for ones that not only test their brainpower but also their emotional resilience. These games challenge them to stay patient and persistent even when the going gets tough, teaching them invaluable lessons in perseverance and self-control.

Of course, balance is key. While digital play has its perks, it shouldn't overshadow real-world interactions. Setting clear limits on screen time ensures that their digital adventures complement, not replace, the hands-on experiences they need to thrive. And why not bring the digital into the real world? If a game has them managing a virtual farm, consider starting a gardening project together. Not only does it reinforce what they've learned, but it also shows them the practical side of their digital fun.

Recommended Digital Tools for Emotional Learning

To really make these ideas work, think about introducing your kids to apps and games like '**Mindful Powers**.' This mindfulness app is perfect for helping kids manage their emotions through fun, story-driven interactions. Another favorite is '**Zoo U**,' which focuses on social skills and emotion recognition in a school-like setting.

But here's the key: don't just hand them the tablet and walk away. Get involved. Play these games with your kids, dive into the characters and storylines, and ask questions that make them think about the emotional aspects of the game. Not only does this help you monitor the content, but it also enriches their learning experience. You'll be right there with them, helping them understand and talk about the emotional skills they're picking up. By watching and discussing their digital interactions, you'll gain insights into their emotional understanding and spot areas where they might need a bit more guidance.

Parental controls can be more than just a barrier—they can be a teaching tool. Explain why some games might not be suitable, and talk about what makes other games a good choice. This helps your kids develop critical thinking about their media choices, encouraging them to look for games that are not only fun but also enriching.

Choosing the right digital games for emotional growth isn't just about filtering content; it's about being an active part of your child's digital world. By picking games that build emotional intelligence, balancing screen time with real-world activities, and engaging in their digital play, you're setting the stage for your kids to become not just good gamers but great individuals. They'll learn empathy, problem-solving, and emotional resilience. These skills picked up in the vibrant, virtual worlds of their games will help them navigate the emotional landscapes of real life.

2.6 Outdoor Activities and Nature's Role in Emotional Learning

Spending time in nature isn't just a nice break—it's an incredible opportunity for emotional growth. Picture this: the soothing rustle of leaves, the joyful chirping of birds, and the tranquil flow of streams. These natural sounds and sights can work wonders in reducing stress and boosting your child's sensory awareness. When boys interact with the environment, they start to understand their emotions better, all while soaking in the peace and beauty of the outdoors.

Gardening, for example, is more than just a hobby. It teaches responsibility and empathy as boys care for plants and watch them grow. Imagine the pride on their faces when they see the fruits of their hard work blooming. Or think about the thrill of a nature scavenger hunt, sparking excitement and discovery, all while boosting their observational skills and mindfulness. These activities help boys learn to manage their emotions in fun and engaging ways.

Mindfulness exercises, like taking quiet walks or watching wildlife, are fantastic for cultivating present-moment awareness. These simple practices can help manage anxiety and stress, improving concentration and creating a calm, focused mind—key ingredients for emotional intelligence. Plus, connecting with nature nurtures empathy and a sense of stewardship toward the environment. Activities that involve observing or gently interacting with animals can help boys develop a sense of connection and responsibility toward all living beings, expanding their empathy beyond just human interactions.

These outdoor experiences provide deep emotional insights and a profound connection to the world. Nature teaches boys about their surroundings, helps them understand their inner selves, and teaches them how to manage their emotions in healthy ways.

Outdoor activities like gardening and scavenger hunts offer unique benefits that nurture emotional skills. Mindfulness in nature improves focus and emotional control, while interacting with the environment fosters empathy and responsibility. These experiences not only enrich boys' emotional intelligence but also their appreciation for nature. As we transition from the lessons of the natural world to more structured environments like classrooms, we continue to explore ways to enhance emotional learning.

CHAPTER HIGHLIGHTS & ACTION POINTS:

- Role of Play in EI Development:

  - Play is crucial for learning empathy, self-regulation, and teamwork.

  - Real-life scenarios, such as helping a peer, demonstrate EI in action.

- Designing Emotionally Intelligent Playtimes:

  - Use games like 'Simon Says' to teach emotional awareness.

  - Choose toys that promote cooperation and emotional learning.

  - Balance structured and unstructured play for comprehensive EI development.

- Games That Grow EI:

  - Board games and sports enhance patience, empathy, and emotional regulation.

  - Storytelling games boost creativity and emotional vocabulary.

- Role of Sports:

  - Sports teach respect, empathy, and self-regulation.

  - Coaches play a crucial role in modeling and teaching EI.

- Creative Arts for Emotional Expression:

- Arts like drawing, music, and drama allow boys to express and understand complex emotions.

- Encourages emotional dialogue and builds self-esteem.

- Digital Games:

  - Select digital games that promote prosocial behavior, problem-solving, and emotional regulation.

  - Balance screen time with real-world activities and engage in digital play together.

- Outdoor Activities:

  - Nature-based activities reduce stress and enhance sensory awareness.

  - Gardening and mindfulness in nature foster responsibility and empathy.

Chapter Three

Emotional Intelligence in the Digital Age

I n a cozy living room, illuminated by the soft glow of evening, a young boy named Theo sits absorbed in a tablet. His fingers swipe deftly across the screen, a look of intense focus etched across his face. This scene, familiar in many homes today, reflects the digital reality of our children's lives. While these devices open up worlds of information and interaction, they also pose unique challenges for nurturing emotional intelligence in the digital age. As we navigate this chapter, let's explore how we can transform screen time from a solitary activity into an opportunity for emotional and social growth.

3.1 Balancing Screen Time and Emotional Well-being

The digital world is a double-edged sword: it offers unprecedented opportunities for learning and connection, yet it also risks overshadowing the real-world interactions crucial for developing emotional intelligence. Excessive screen time can reduce face-to-face interactions, which are essential for learning nuanced emotional cues like body language and tone of voice. Over time, this can dampen a child's ability to empathize and read social situations correctly. Moreover, digital devices' immediate gratification may impair a child's ability to deal with delayed gratification and frustration, potentially impacting their emotional regulation skills.

Setting healthy boundaries around screen time is essential, and it begins with understanding that not all screen time is created equal. As a caregiver, distinguishing between passive consumption and interactive use can guide you in setting these limits effectively. For younger children, the American Academy of Pediatrics suggests no more than one hour of quality programming per day, while for older children, the focus shifts towards ensuring that digital engagements do not replace time needed for sleep, physical activities, and other behaviors essential to health. Incorporate these guidelines thoughtfully within your family's routine, considering your child's developmental needs and the values you want to cultivate. For instance, you might decide that devices must be turned off at least an hour before bedtime to ensure sound sleep or that mealtimes are tech-free zones to encourage family discussions.

Quality Over Quantity

Prioritize high-quality digital content contributing to your child's emotional and intellectual growth. Educational apps and games that encourage problem-solving and creativity can be beneficial, but active engagement is key. Look for apps where children are creators, not just consumers. Programs that simulate real-world activities like cooking, building, or even coding can provide engaging, hands-on learning experiences that develop technical skills, planning, problem-solving, and patience.

Engaging in Digital Content Together

One of the most effective ways to enhance the benefits of screen time is to engage in digital activities together. This could be as simple as discussing the storyline of a video game, watching a documentary together, or even co-creating digital art or music. This shared screen time allows you to monitor the content and opens up opportunities for rich, meaningful discussions that reinforce learning and bond formation. For example, after playing an educational game together, you might discuss the characters' emotions or the moral dilemmas they faced. This helps in understanding the content at a deeper level and connecting it to real-life emotional scenarios.

Interactive Element: Family Digital Activity Planner

To help you implement these strategies, consider using the 'Family Digital Activity Planner.' This tool can help you plan and track digital activities that are *engaging, educational, and emotionally enriching*. It can serve as a guide to balancing screen time across the week, ensuring a healthy mix of solo and shared activities, and keeping an eye on the quality of content your child is engaging with.

Navigating the digital landscape effectively requires a balanced approach that leverages the educational potential of digital tools while nurturing essential real-world experiences for emotional development. By establishing clear boundaries, prioritizing high-quality content, and engaging with digital media together, we can ensure our children's online activities support their emotional well-being. As we delve into the complexities of emotional intelligence in the digital age, remember that our crucial roles as mentors and co-learners help our children confidently and responsibly explore the digital world.

3.2 Social Media: The Emotional Intelligence Perspective

In today's digital age, boys are navigating their social environments through social media in unprecedented ways. As they engage with content across platforms, they're consuming information and crafting their identities, relationships, and emotional well-being. Teaching them to use social media with emotional intelligence is essential for their overall development, ensuring they grow into emotionally healthy and digitally savvy individuals.

Navigating social media with emotional intelligence requires understanding its role as both a self-expression and learning tool, and a source of comparison, cyberbullying, and unrealistic expectations that can undermine boys' self-esteem and emotional health. Guiding boys towards mindful social media use involves open discussions about their online intentions and impacts, teaching them to differentiate between meaningful connections and the passive consumption of idealized content. Encouraging them to be selective in their online interactions promotes a digital environment conducive to positive emotional growth.

Teaching digital empathy is crucial for fostering a respectful and caring online community. It goes beyond just understanding what someone posts—it's about grasping the emotions and context behind their digital interactions. For example, when a friend shares a personal achievement, it's a chance to talk about feeling proud and how to show support. On the flip side, if someone posts about a tough time, it's an opportunity to discuss compassion and how to offer comfort online. Role-playing helps here: creating hypothetical social media situations and discussing different responses can show boys the impact of their words and actions online and improve their ability to empathize.

Social media literacy is also essential. It means understanding the ins and outs of online communication, privacy settings, and knowing that what they post online can last forever. Start these conversations early, using simple explanations about personal information and why it's crucial to keep certain details private. For example, explaining that sharing a location online is like giving a physical key to a stranger might help a young boy understand why it's important to be careful. Regular talks about online safety, how social media algorithms work, and how they can shape what they see will give them the knowledge to navigate social media safely and smartly.

Lastly, modeling positive social media behavior is crucial. Show empathy, respect, and discretion online to set an example for boys. Talk openly about your social media choices, like handling disagreements and protecting privacy. These conversations reinforce emotional intelligence skills. Equip boys to navigate social media thoughtfully, promoting mindfulness, empathy, and digital literacy. These abilities help them navigate the online world with the same compassion and wisdom they use offline.

3.3 Digital Empathy: Teaching Kids to Navigate Online Spaces

In the vast expanse of the digital universe, where interactions can be as fleeting as they are profound, the concept of digital empathy becomes not just relevant but necessary. Digital empathy is the ability to understand and share the feelings of others through digital communication. It's about reading between the lines of a text message, sensing the emotions behind a social media post, and responding with sensitivity and awareness. This kind of empathy ensures that online interactions are not just information transactions but exchanges imbued with human warmth and understanding.

Understanding digital empathy begins with recognizing that online interactions, though often devoid of physical presence, are deeply emotional. When a boy comments on a friend's post or responds to a message, he's engaging in an emotional exchange. Teaching him to pause and consider the tone and content of his responses is crucial. It's about helping him understand that behind every profile picture and username is a real person with feelings that can be hurt or uplifted by his words. For instance, if a friend shares a post about losing a pet, teaching him to send a message of condolence that acknowledges the pain **"I'm so sorry about your dog. It must be really tough."** rather than a generic or dismissive response **"That's life!"** shows a deep level of digital empathy.

Cyberbullying shows why emotional intelligence and digital empathy are so important. The anonymity of the internet can make it easy to forget the impact of our actions. Emotional intelligence helps boys understand this and stand up against bullying. Talk to them about the emotional consequences of cyberbullying so they see the real-world effects of their words. This helps them learn to interact online with care and consideration.

Online Compassion Projects

Engaging boys in online compassion projects or positive messaging campaigns can transform them. Activities like starting a positivity blog or organizing virtual events promote kindness and empathy. These activities spread positivity and allow boys to experience the impact of leading with empathy and compassion in the digital realm.

Communicating empathetically online is a skill that boys will carry into adulthood, making its teaching vital. Start with the basics of online communication etiquette: think before you click, re-read before you send, and choose words that convey respect and kindness. Teach them to use language that shows consideration for others' feelings. For example, instead of saying **"That's wrong,"** they could say, **"I see it differently, here's my perspective."** Encouraging emojis and punctuation can also help convey tone and prevent misunderstandings. For instance, a simple smiley face can soften a critique, making it feel friendlier. Moreover, respecting differences online—whether they are of opinion, culture, or interest—reinforces the practice of empathy. It's about acknowledging that everyone has the right to feel safe and respected in digital spaces, just as they do in physical ones.

Teaching digital empathy goes beyond instructing boys on proper online behavior; it's about helping them understand and value the emotions that connect us. By navigating online spaces with empathy and respect, they become better digital citizens and enhance their emotional intelligence. These skills ensure that as they scroll, click, and comment, they do so with an awareness that their words can touch hearts and positively shape the digital world.

3.4 Video Games and Emotional Resilience

Video games, often criticized, actually teach emotional resilience. When boys play, they face challenges and setbacks, building perseverance and adaptability that translate into real-world determination.

Games mimic real-life pressures—decision-making, complex environments, and time-sensitive puzzles—providing a safe space to practice stress responses and coping skills. Choosing the right games is key; look for those that balance challenge and achievability to encourage problem-solving and a growth mindset.

Talking about gameplay experiences can help boys manage frustration and turn virtual challenges into real-life lessons. Parent-child gaming sessions offer unique opportunities to model and discuss emotional management and resilience strategies. These interactions go beyond entertainment, allowing for direct observation and guidance, celebrating achievements, and strengthening bonds through shared experiences of joy and mutual disappointment. This collaborative play modernizes traditional resilience training, equipping boys with the confidence and perseverance to face life's challenges. Through video games, boys develop the emotional skills essential for navigating real-world complexities.

3.5 Online Bullying: Building Emotional Strength

In the digital world, online bullying can cast a shadow over social media and gaming. Understanding its emotional impact is crucial. For boys navigating these spaces, the anonymity of screens can make them targets or, regrettably, bullies. Being bullied online can lead to feelings of isolation, anxiety, and low self-esteem, affecting all areas of their life.

To tackle this, boys need a toolkit of good intentions and practical strategies. Teach them the importance of seeking help—encourage them to talk to a trusted adult like a parent, teacher, or counselor for support. They should know it's okay to ask for help. Show them how to use reporting features on social media and games to block or report bullies, giving them control over the situation and boosting their confidence.

Practicing digital empathy is a powerful way to combat online bullying. Encourage boys to understand and consider the feelings of others, making them advocates for positivity. Role-playing online scenarios can help—discuss how to respond if they witness bullying. For instance, discussing how to respond if they witness bullying online can prepare them to act thoughtfully. Knowing how to express support for the victims and report incidents can make a significant difference.

Preventative Measures for Caregivers

In today's digital world, as caregivers, we face unique challenges in keeping our children safe. Open communication is key—regularly talking about online activities helps us understand the social dynamics they're navigating. We need to set clear rules for internet use to provide structure and safety, and staying informed about social media trends helps us discuss privacy settings and online etiquette with them.

Encouraging offline relationships and activities like sports or clubs is important for building a supportive community for our boys. These real-world connections offer emotional support, buffering the negative impacts of online negativity.

By fostering supportive online and offline networks, we can protect our boys from online bullying and empower them to stand against it. These lessons in empathy and resilience keep them safe and also contribute to creating a more positive world.

CHAPTER HIGHLIGHTS & ACTION POINTS:

- Balancing Screen Time and Emotional Well-being

  - Understand how excessive screen time impacts emotional intelligence.

  - Establish healthy boundaries by prioritizing quality over quantity in digital content.

  - Incorporate shared screen time activities to bond and discuss emotions and real-life situations.

- Engaging in Digital Content Together

  - Strengthen the benefits of screen time by joining your child in digital activities.

  - Use these moments to monitor content, have meaningful discussions, and reinforce learning.

  - Share your insights and experiences to deepen understanding and connection.

- Family Digital Activity Planner

  - Create a 'Family Digital Activity Planner' to schedule enriching digital activities.

  - Balance solo and shared activities to promote emotional growth and connection.

  - Track your child's digital experiences to ensure quality content consumption.

- Teaching Digital Empathy

  - Foster empathy by discussing the emotions and context

behind online interactions.

- Role-play different scenarios to illustrate the impact of words and actions online.

- Educate on social media etiquette and safety, drawing from personal experiences and values.

- Modeling Positive Social Media Behavior

  - Lead by example in demonstrating empathy, respect, and discretion online.

  - Share your thought process and decision-making regarding social media choices.

  - Equip your child with essential skills like mindfulness and digital literacy through open discussions and practical guidance.

Chapter Four

──────────────

Grit and Resilience: The Warriors' Path

Picture a young boy, his determination evident as he painstakingly constructs a complex puzzle. Each piece that slots into place triggers a visible surge of satisfaction, while those that don't seem to fit prompt a momentary frown, a brief flicker of frustration. Yet, he persists, his eyes scanning, his mind whirring until he uncovers the right fit. This seemingly insignificant scene is, in fact, a potent metaphor for the heart of grit—a quality that intertwines perseverance with passion, propelling one to overcome obstacles in pursuit of long-term goals. In this chapter, we unravel the layers of grit and resilience in child development, examining how these essential traits can be nurtured, from the challenges of the playground to life's significant hurdles.

4.1 The Science of Grit in Child Development

Defining Grit in Children

Grit in children is like the invisible muscle that flexes itself when challenges arise. It's the perseverance to keep going when a task gets tough and the passion that fuels long-term commitments, regardless of setbacks. For young boys, developing grit can mean persisting with a complex math problem, improving a sports skill, or completing a lengthy project over several weeks or months. This quality isn't about sprinting; it's the marathon runner in them, setting a pace to reach a distant finish line with determination and focus.

Biological and Environmental Influences

Understanding grit in boys involves both their natural traits and the environment we create for them. Some kids are naturally more persistent, but much of their resilience comes from how we, as parents, caregivers, or teachers, support them. Our reactions to their setbacks and successes, the opportunities we give them to face challenges, and how we model perseverance all contribute significantly. For example, encouraging kids to try new things and viewing failures as learning experiences helps them develop grit.

Measuring Grit

Assessing grit and resilience in kids can seem tricky, like measuring the wind with a ruler, but there are practical ways to do it. We can observe how children stick with tasks, getting insights from teachers or caregivers about their persistence. Tools like the "Grit Scale for Children" help gauge their determination to achieve long-term goals with passion. These methods are essential for understanding where your child is now and tracking their growth, helping you support their development every step of the way.

Enhancing Grit through Experience

Building grit is all about the experiences we gather, both structured and unstructured. Whether it's joining a sports team, taking music lessons, or sticking to a study routine, these structured activities teach us discipline and the joy of achieving our goals through hard work. But it's not just about schedules and plans; unstructured experiences are just as important. Whether it's exploring new hobbies or facing unexpected challenges, these moments push us to adapt, think on our feet, and handle frustrations without a roadmap. Every experience, big or small, planned or spontaneous, shapes our resilient mindset and helps us grow our grit.

Interactive Element: Grit Growth Journal

Have you noticed grit being demonstrated by your son lately? To practically apply these concepts and monitor progress, consider maintaining a "Grit Growth Journal" for or with the boys you guide. This journal can serve as a tool to record daily or weekly challenges, the strategies used to overcome them, and reflections on what was learned. It's a way to visualize progress and setbacks in a tangible form. It can be an incredibly motivating tool, showing that growth often comes in waves, with ups and downs, rather than a straight line. This activity reinforces the lessons of perseverance and passion. It makes developing grit a conscious, reflective practice integrated into daily life.

As we continue to explore the multifaceted nature of grit and resilience, remember that these traits are not just about enduring but thriving. They're about equipping boys with the mindset and tools to face life's challenges with determination and an understanding that every hurdle overcome is a step towards greater strength and achievement. Let's keep building that resilience, one challenge at a time.

4.2 Challenges That Build Resilience

Raising boys to be resilient warriors in life involves introducing them to various challenges that naturally foster their ability to bounce back and persevere. These challenges, tailored to their age and development stage, serve as the building blocks of resilience, preparing them for the complexities of adult responsibilities and relationships. For the little ones, these challenges might be as simple as learning to tie their shoes or cleaning up their room without assistance. These tasks, while mundane, teach them that effort leads to achievement. As boys grow, the complexity of these challenges should evolve, incorporating tasks like managing a weekly allowance or completing a group project at school. These experiences push them to develop planning skills, teamwork, and the ability to handle the occasional disappointment when things don't go as planned.

With its inherent challenges and boundless beauty, the natural world offers a perfect backdrop for developing resilience. Nature is unpredictable, and operating within it requires an inevitable surrender to the elements, whether it's weather changes during a camping trip or the physical demands of a hike. Each outdoor adventure can teach valuable lessons in adaptability and perseverance. For instance, when my son asked me to teach him how to read the compass and map, I thought to myself this was a perfect opportunity to start instilling problem-solving skills and confidence to make decisions in uncertain situations. Similarly, dealing with the unexpected, like a sudden rainstorm or a missed trail marker, teaches boys to stay calm under pressure and look for solutions rather than dwelling on the problem.

Sports and physical activities offer more than just fun; they're classrooms for life. Every moment on the field teaches boys about teamwork, success, and failure, showing them that setbacks are opportunities for growth. Reflecting on each game builds a habit of self-improvement, while the physical demands toughen them up mentally and physically.

Friendships are another arena for resilience. From making new friends to handling conflicts, each interaction teaches valuable communication skills and empathy. Practicing these skills through role-playing, gives them a chance to rehearse tricky situations in a safe space. Whether it's learning how to join a game at the park or handling conflict with a friend, these experiences build their confidence and social skills.

Exposing boys to diverse challenges builds resilience, strengthening their character with each task conquered. It's about showing them that challenges are chances to grow stronger and wiser, whether through everyday tasks, nature's unpredictability, sports discipline, or navigating friendships.

4.3 Failure as a Stepping Stone to Resilience

In raising resilient boys, it's vital to reshape their perspective on failure. Rather than viewing it as a setback, they should see it as a stepping stone—a crucial part of the learning process. This shift in mindset, from seeing failure as a barrier to embracing it as an opportunity for growth, is powerful. When boys understand that every misstep is a chance to learn, they approach challenges with confidence. They start to see themselves as problem solvers and innovators, willing to take risks and explore new ideas, knowing that each experience contributes to their growth.

Creating a Safe Space for Failure

Creating environments that encourage risk-taking and learning from failures is vital. This can be as simple as the language used when discussing outcomes. For example, instead of saying, "That didn't work out well, did it?" you might say, **"What did we learn from this experience?"** Such questions emphasize learning over judgment, promoting a culture where boys feel safe to try new things without fear of ridicule or punishment. At home or in the classroom, this might look like celebrating **'brave tries'** or **'creative attempts,'** regardless of the outcome. It's about making your home or classroom a laboratory for experimentation, where 'failures' are seen as part of the discovery process.

Offering specific feedback instead of broad praise enables boys to discern which strategies are effective and which require refinement. This strategy cultivates their ability to critically evaluate their efforts, leading to a deeper comprehension of success and failure. For example, dissecting the reasons behind a science project's unexpected results and collaboratively exploring modifications to the hypothesis or methodology transforms a setback into a constructive lesson.

Teaching Emotional Coping Skills for Failure

Equipping boys with emotional coping strategies is crucial for managing the disappointment and frustration that often follow setbacks. Techniques like *deep breathing, journaling, and open discussions about their feelings* are vital for effective emotion regulation. These practices empower boys to confront challenges directly, learn from them, and advance with resilience. Additionally, integrating *structured reflection* after setbacks can significantly improve their learning from these experiences. Boys develop a deeper understanding of navigating obstacles by reviewing what succeeded and failed and identifying adjustments for future attempts. Guiding them through questions such as, **"What was the most challenging part of this task?"** and "**How did you cope when things didn't go as planned?"** not only enhances their ability to express their experiences and emotions but also fosters a reflective habit that improves both emotional well-being and task performance in subsequent challenges.

Real-life Examples of Successful Failures

Sharing stories of well-known figures who have failed and achieved great success can also be incredibly motivating. Consider figures like **Thomas Edison**, whose numerous failed attempts at creating a light bulb culminated in a revolutionary invention. Or **J.K. Rowling**, who was rejected by multiple publishers before finding one who would take a chance on Harry Potter. These stories highlight that the path to success isn't straight; it's filled with bumps and detours, all of which are valuable. Discussing these examples helps boys understand that everyone, no matter how successful, experiences setbacks—what matters is how they respond to them.

Incorporating these strategies into your daily interactions can transform boys' views on failure and success, fostering resilience that empowers them to advance from setbacks. By creating a learning environment that embraces failure, teaching emotional coping techniques, and sharing stories of successful failures, you provide boys with essential tools for navigating life's challenges with confidence and perseverance.

4.4 Cultivating a Growth Mindset in Boys

Understanding the difference between a fixed mindset and a growth mindset can completely change how boys approach challenges and learning. A fixed mindset makes them believe that their talents and intelligence are set in stone, leading to a fear of failure. On the other hand, a growth mindset sees challenges as opportunities to develop and expand their abilities. It teaches boys that effort and perseverance can enhance their skills, showing them the importance of embracing each step as a chance to grow beyond their current limits.

The way we deliver praise plays a big role in nurturing a growth mindset in boys. Instead of just praising innate ability, we should focus on praising their effort. For instance, rather than saying, "You're so smart," we might say, **"I'm really proud of how hard you worked on this."** This kind of feedback encourages boys to keep pushing themselves and understand that intelligence can be developed through dedication and hard work. Encouraging them to take on challenges is also crucial. We should urge them to step out of their comfort zones, try new things, and not back down from tasks that seem tough. When they realize that overcoming obstacles is just part of the learning process, they're more likely to keep going, even

when things get difficult.

Changing how boys view criticism and setbacks is essential for building a growth mindset. Instead of seeing criticism as a personal attack, they should see it as an opportunity to grow. Teaching them to embrace feedback as a way to improve themselves fosters resilience and a positive attitude toward challenges. Learning to handle setbacks with grace and seeing them as chances to learn and improve is vital for nurturing a strong growth mindset.

Role Models of Growth Mindset

Highlighting role models who exemplify a growth mindset can be incredibly inspiring. Consider figures like **Albert Einstein**, who famously said, "It's not that I'm so smart, it's just that I stay with problems longer." Or, contemporary figures like **Elon Musk**, who, despite numerous setbacks, continues to pursue his goals with enthusiasm. These stories can be powerful motivators, showing boys that perseverance and a willingness to learn from mistakes are common threads among successful individuals. Discussing the challenges and setbacks these figures faced and how they were used as stepping stones to success can help boys understand that difficulties are just part of the journey to achievement.

> "It's not that I'm so smart, it's just that I stay with problems longer." -Albert Einstein

Activities to Encourage Growth Mindset Thinking

To bring the idea of a growth mindset to life, get boys involved in setting goals and tracking their progress. Creating a **"progress journal"** can be a great way for them to jot down their learning goals and see how they're doing week by week or month by month. It's a hands-on way for them to visualize their growth and develop a purposeful approach to learning. Another fun activity is to give them *problem-solving challenges* that are just a bit above their current abilities. Whether it's tackling academic puzzles or learning practical life skills, the goal is to find that sweet spot where they can succeed with effort but still feel challenged. By trying different strategies and reflecting on their attempts, they learn that abilities can grow with practice and perseverance.

Building a growth mindset is all about changing how boys see their own abilities and the importance of effort in achieving success. By praising their effort, encouraging them to take on challenges, teaching them to learn from criticism, and sharing stories of people who embody a growth mindset, you're giving them the tools to approach life with a mindset focused on learning and growing. It's about shifting their mindset from asking "Can I do this?" to asking **"How will I do this?"**—opening up a world of possibilities for personal and academic growth.

4.5 Perseverance: Stories and Role Models

Inspiring Stories of Perseverance

Picture the unwavering determination of individuals who faced daunting obstacles head-on, yet refused to yield. Think of **Malala Yousafzai**, bravely advocating for education in a Taliban-controlled region despite grave threats. After surviving a near-fatal attack, she emerged stronger, becoming a global voice for education and women's rights, earning the Nobel Peace Prize. Her resilience inspires millions worldwide.

Consider **Chris Gardner**, portrayed in **"The Pursuit of Happiness."** Faced with homelessness and sole custody of his son, Gardner persisted through immense challenges, striving for a better life. His story is a testament to the power of resilience, turning despair into hope and adversity into triumph.

These tales resonate deeply, teaching boys the importance of facing life's storms with resilience. They show that despite overwhelming odds, staying focused on goals and persevering through difficulties can lead to extraordinary outcomes.

Using Literature and Media

Books, movies, and other media are treasure troves of tales that embody perseverance and resilience. Take **"Hatchet" by Gary Paulsen,** where a young boy's survival in the wild showcases the power of wit and determination. Or consider **"October Sky,"** depicting a boy's unwavering pursuit of rocketry dreams despite setbacks and naysayers.

These stories offer more than entertainment; they're lessons in resilience. They show boys how characters overcome challenges, inspiring them to tackle their own obstacles with determination. Discussing these stories deepens their impact, encouraging boys to reflect on applying similar perseverance in their lives.

By immersing boys in diverse narratives and relatable role models, you show them that resilience means thriving despite adversity. It's about embracing challenges as growth opportunities and understanding setbacks as setups for comebacks. Through these stories, boys learn that perseverance is the key to success, propelling them forward with unwavering determination.

4.6 Rewarding Effort Over Achievement

Understanding the value of effort over mere achievement is like tending a garden; it's not just about the blooming flowers but the care and attention that led to their growth. When you celebrate a child's effort, you validate the journey toward an outcome, fostering resilience and a love for learning. Praising effort helps boys grasp that growth comes through persistence and hard work, rather than innate talent alone.

Reward systems emphasizing effort and improvement can transform how boys approach challenges. For instance, in a classroom, you might track completed assignments alongside grades based on a student's dedication and approach. At home, praising attempts to tackle difficult tasks, even if they're not initially successful, can be equally impactful. These systems highlight the often unseen aspects of learning, like critical thinking and perseverance.

Case Studies: Shifting Focus from Outcome to Effort

Let's dive into some real-life examples where emphasizing effort led to remarkable transformations. Consider the case of a middle school math class that shifted its reward system from test scores to effort indicators, such as persistence in problem-solving and seeking out additional resources when stuck. Over the semester, the students' math scores improved, and their overall engagement and attitudes toward learning math transformed. They were more willing to tackle complex problems and less fearful of making mistakes, knowing their efforts would be recognized and celebrated regardless of the outcome.

Another case involved a youth soccer coach who decided to focus less on winning games and more on teamwork, effort, and sportsmanship. Each player was praised for actions that showed effort and collaboration, such as making a great pass or encouraging a teammate, rather than just scoring goals. This approach improved the team's cohesion and sportsmanship and led to better overall performance in tournaments. Players were more motivated to contribute to the team's success in various ways, knowing their efforts were seen and valued.

Encouraging boys to assess their own progress is key to nurturing independence and self-drive. By setting personal goals and reflecting on achievements and areas for growth, they become more engaged in their learning journey. Whether through reflection sessions or keeping a personal journal, these habits deepen their understanding of learning processes and encourage them to tackle challenges head-on. This self-awareness strengthens their perseverance and enhances their overall learning experience.

As we wrap up our discussion on the transformative power of valuing effort, we highlight the shift toward a growth-centered mindset. This crucial change fosters resilience, motivation, and independence, arming boys with the confidence and curiosity essential for their future. Emphasizing effort over outcomes is critical to building resilience and perseverance, significantly boosting boys' educational and personal growth. This perspective prepares them to face life's challenges with determination and creativity. Our aim is to create environments that cherish learning and personal development above mere success.

CHAPTER HIGHLIGHTS & ACTION POINTS:

- Defining Grit:

  - Grit is perseverance and passion crucial for long-term goals.

  - It's influenced by both innate traits and environmental factors.

- Measuring and Enhancing Grit:

  - Practical methods for assessing and nurturing grit include exposing them to a new hobby, sport, or music, and observing them stick to it with perseverance.

  - Structured and unstructured experiences contribute to grit development.

- Interactive Tool: Start a Grit Growth Journal

  - Record challenges, strategies, and reflections to visualize progress.

- Challenges That Build Resilience:

  - Nature, sports, friendships, and diverse experiences shape resilience.

  - Introduce various challenges, tailor tasks to age and interests.

- Failure as a Stepping Stone:

  - Reshaping perspectives on failure as opportunities for growth.

  - Teach emotional coping skills and create safe spaces for

failure.

- Cultivating a Growth Mindset:

  - Encourage effort over innate ability and embrace challenges.

- Perseverance: Stories and Role Models:

  - Praise effort and share inspiring stories from real-life examples and literature.

- Rewarding Effort Over Achievement:

  - Implement reward systems emphasizing effort and improvement.

  - Celebrate attempts and persistence.

Make a Difference with Your Review

Unlock the Power of Generosity

> "Empathy is about finding echoes of another person in yourself." - Mohsin Hamid

People who give without expectation live longer, happier lives and feel more fulfilled. So if we've got a shot at that during our time together, I'm going to try my best.

To make that happen, I have a question for you...

Would you help someone you've never met, even if you never got credit for it?

Who is this person you ask? They are like you. Or, at least, like you used to be. Less experienced, wanting to make a difference, and needing help, but not sure where to look.

Our mission is to make Raising Warriors: Nurturing Boys to be Emotionally Intelligent and Mentally Strong accessible to everyone. Everything I do stems from that mission. And, the only way for me to accomplish that mission is by reaching...well...everyone.

This is where you come in. Most people do, in fact, judge a book by its cover (and its reviews). So here's my ask on behalf of a struggling parent or caregiver you've never met:

Please help that parent or caregiver by leaving this book a review.

Your gift costs no money and less than 60 seconds to make real, but can change a fellow parent or caregiver's life forever. Your review could help...

...one more parent raise an emotionally intelligent son.

...one more caregiver find the support they need.

...one more family strengthen their bonds.

...one more child grow into a strong, empathetic adult.

...one more dream come true.

To get that 'feel good' feeling and help this person for real, all you have to do is...and it takes less than 60 seconds...

leave a review.

Simply scan the QR code below to leave your review:

SCAN ME

If you feel good about helping a faceless parent, you are my kind of person. Welcome to the club. You're one of us.

I'm that much more excited to help you build your son's mental strength & emotional intelligence faster and easier than you can possibly imagine. You'll love the strategies and insights I'm about to share in the coming chapters.

Thank you from the bottom of my heart.

-Kaye Buenaventure

PS - Fun fact: If you provide something of value to another person, it makes you more valuable to them. If you'd like goodwill straight from another parent or caregiver - and you believe this book will help them - send this book their way.

_____

Chapter Five

Strategies for Overcoming Common Challenges

I magine watching a group of young boys at the park. They are at that tender age where friendships are starting to mean more than just shared toys and games. One boy, let's call him Andy, finds himself facing a dilemma when his friends dare him to climb up a high fence. It's clear he's hesitant, his feet shuffling in the dirt and his eyes flickering with uncertainty. This scene, while simple, captures the essence of peer pressure—a dynamic every young boy navigates as he grows. In this chapter, we'll explore how we can equip boys like Andy with the emotional intelligence tools they need to handle such situations with confidence and integrity.

5.1 Navigating Peer Pressure with Emotional Intelligence

Understanding the Dynamics of Peer Pressure

Peer pressure is not just about daring feats at the park; it's a complex psychological phenomenon that can influence a boy's choices about everything, from what he wears to how he behaves in and out of school. This pressure can be overt, as in the case of a direct challenge or dare, or it can be subtler, manifesting through non-verbal cues and the silent weight of expectations. Understanding this dynamic is crucial because it sets the stage for how boys like Andy can learn to respond. It's about recognizing that peer pressure can sometimes push boys away from their true preferences and values, nudging them towards actions they might regret. By breaking down these interactions, we can help boys identify when they're being influenced and empower them to make decisions that align with their values.

Tools for Resisting Negative Peer Influence

Equipping boys with the tools to resist negative peer influence starts with fostering strong self-esteem and a clear sense of their values. One effective verbal strategy is teaching them to assertively communicate their stance without aggression or passivity. Phrases like **"I don't think that's a good idea"** or **"I'm not comfortable doing this"** are simple yet powerful tools boys can use. Non-verbal strategies are equally important. Body language that conveys confidence, such as maintaining eye contact and standing firm, can often speak louder than words. These tools help boys stand up for themselves and teach them the importance of respecting their limits and listening to their internal compass.

Role-Playing Scenarios

Role-playing is an invaluable method for practicing these responses in a safe environment. Boys can rehearse how they might react in real life by simulating various peer pressure scenarios. For example, role-playing a situation where a group of friends encourages cheating on a test can allow boys to practice saying no and suggesting an alternative, like forming a study group. These rehearsals can help diminish the anxiety associated with standing up to peers, making it more likely that they'll act according to their values when the situation arises.

Building a Supportive Peer Network

Lastly, cultivating a supportive peer network is crucial. Encourage boys to seek friendships with peers who share similar values and interests, as these friends are more likely to provide positive reinforcement and less likely to exert harmful pressure. Activities like team sports, clubs, or community service projects can be great avenues for meeting like-minded peers. Additionally, fostering an environment where boys feel comfortable discussing their friendships with adults can provide them with guidance and reassurance, helping them confidently navigate their social circles.

Interactive Element: Friendship Circle Evaluation

A practical tool to implement is the "Friendship Circle Evaluation." This exercise involves boys mapping out their social connections in concentric circles, with the innermost circle for closest friends and outer circles for acquaintances. This visual tool can help them reflect on the influence different peers have on them and assess whether these relationships are supportive or challenging. It encourages boys to think critically about who they choose to spend time with and why, reinforcing the importance of nurturing positive and healthy relationships.

In navigating the complexities of peer pressure with emotional intelligence, the goal is not just to teach boys how to say no, but to empower them to make choices that reflect their true selves. It's about helping them develop the confidence to stand alone when necessary and the wisdom to choose friends who will stand by them, not just when it's easy but especially when it's hard. As we continue to explore strategies for overcoming common challenges, remember that each lesson in emotional intelligence helps boys manage the pressures of today and equips them for the broader challenges of tomorrow.

5.2 Dealing with Anger: Strategies for Boys

Let's talk about a typical scenario you might have witnessed: a young boy at a playground gets pushed off the slide and immediately lashes out, his face turning red, hands balling into fists. It's a natural response to a provoking situation but also a teachable moment about managing anger. Anger, like any other emotion, is entirely normal, but learning to handle it healthily is crucial for boys as they grow into adulthood. This part of our discussion focuses on identifying what triggers anger, expressing it constructively, and learning techniques to manage it effectively.

Recognizing Triggers

First things first, helping boys recognize what triggers their anger is important. It's about making them aware of the specific situations, actions, or words that spark their anger. This awareness is the first step in managing their responses. For instance, a boy might notice that he feels particularly angry when he's interrupted while speaking or when he feels ignored. By helping them make these observations, you're equipping them with the knowledge to anticipate and prepare for these situations. This can be done through regular discussions about their day or specific incidents where they felt angry. Questions like, **"What were you doing right before you felt angry?"** or **"How did your body feel when you got angry?"** can help boys connect physical sensations and contexts with their emotions.

Healthy Expression of Anger

Once boys understand their triggers, teaching them healthy ways to express their anger is crucial. Suppressing anger is neither healthy nor practical; instead, expressing it in non-destructive ways can prevent it from escalating and negatively affecting relationships.

Teach boys to use *"I" statements* that focus on their feelings rather than blaming others. For example, instead of saying, **"You made me angry,"** they could say, **"I felt angry when this happened."** This small shift helps them express their feelings clearly. It prevents the other person from becoming defensive, paving the way for a constructive conversation. Encouraging them to draw or write about their feelings can also provide a safe outlet for their emotions. These methods allow boys to vent without causing harm to themselves or others, helping them understand that while they can't always control what happens to them, they can control how they respond.

Anger Management Techniques

Practical anger management techniques are essential for boys to have in their emotional toolkit. Techniques such as deep breathing, counting to ten, or engaging in physical activity like running or squeezing a stress ball can help manage the physiological response to anger. For example, teaching boys to take deep breaths involves inhaling slowly through the nose, holding the breath for a few seconds, and then exhaling slowly through the mouth. This simple exercise can have a calming effect on the nervous system and can quickly diffuse anger. Encouraging physical activities like sports can also provide a healthy outlet for their energy and reduce the intensity of their anger. Integrating these techniques into daily routines, perhaps through a morning or after-school routine, can make them more accessible and natural for boys to use when they feel angry.

Role of Adults in Modeling Anger Management

Lastly, your role as an adult in modeling effective anger management cannot be overstated. Children learn a lot from observing the adults in their lives. Suppose they see you managing your anger through calm discussion and healthy outlets. In that case, they are more likely to emulate these behaviors. When you feel angry, verbalize your emotion and let them see how you handle it constructively. For instance, if a situation at work upsets you, you might say, **"I felt really angry when my work was criticized today, but I took some deep breaths and spoke to my colleague about how we can improve the project."** This not only shows them that it's normal to feel angry but also provides a real-life example of handling anger in a healthy way.

Through these discussions and strategies, we aim to equip boys with the understanding that anger is a normal part of life and the tools and techniques to manage it constructively. By recognizing triggers, expressing anger healthily, learning practical management techniques, and seeing these modeled by adults, boys can develop robust emotional intelligence that helps them navigate the playground and beyond.

5.3 Managing Anxiety and Stress in Boys

Anxiety and stress aren't just adult concerns; they touch the lives of boys, too, often in ways we might not immediately recognize. Picture a young boy sitting quietly in the corner of a bustling classroom. His silence might go unnoticed amidst the chatter, but his mind could be swirling with worries—from academic pressures to social dynamics. Understanding how stress and anxiety manifest in boys is the first step toward helping them navigate these challenges effectively.

Identifying Symptoms of Anxiety and Stress

Unlike adults, who can articulate their feelings more clearly, boys might display anxiety and stress through various behaviors that can be mistakenly overlooked as mere mischief or disobedience. Common signs include unexplained irritability, frequent headaches or stomachaches, changes in eating habits, or an unusual decline in academic performance. They might also exhibit signs of withdrawal, opting to stay alone rather than with friends or show a sudden lack of interest in activities they previously enjoyed. Sleep disturbances, such as trouble falling asleep or frequent nightmares, can also be indicators of underlying anxiety or stress. It's crucial for you, as caregivers and educators, to be attuned to these subtle cues, as they can be the first signs that a boy is struggling with anxiety or stress.

Techniques for Reducing Anxiety

Once we recognize the signs, the next step is to equip boys with practical techniques to manage their anxiety. *Mindfulness exercises* are a great starting point. Simple practices like mindful breathing or focusing on sensory experiences (like the feel of a soft ball or the sound of music) can help calm the mind and bring a sense of grounding in moments of anxiety. Another powerful tool is *journaling*, which allows boys to express their thoughts and emotions freely on paper. This can be particularly helpful for those who might not feel comfortable speaking about their feelings yet. *Structured problem-solving* is another technique that can empower boys to take charge of what's causing them stress. For instance, if a looming test is the source of anxiety, breaking down study tasks into manageable chunks and scheduling them can help alleviate overwhelming feelings.

Creating a Calm Environment

The environment around boys plays a critical role in influencing their stress levels. Creating a calm, organized space where boys can retreat and recharge at home can make a significant difference. This might mean setting up a dedicated quiet corner with comforting items like soft pillows, books, or stress-relief toys. In classrooms, reducing sensory overload can be beneficial. This could involve minimizing loud noises or clutter, which can exacerbate feelings of anxiety. Also, establishing a predictable routine can provide a sense of security, reducing anxiety that comes from uncertainty. Regular routines like predictable homework times, regular meal times, and a bedtime routine can provide a comforting structure.

Encouraging Open Conversations About Feelings

Perhaps one of the most impactful ways to manage anxiety and stress in boys is fostering an environment where they feel safe to express their feelings. This involves more than just giving them space to talk; it's about creating an atmosphere of non-judgment and empathy. Start conversations about feelings by sharing your experiences with stress or anxiety in a relatable way. Use language that's easy for boys to understand and encourage them to describe what they're feeling and why they think they feel that way. This helps them develop a vocabulary for their emotions and enhances their emotional intelligence over time. Reinforce that experiencing stress and anxiety is normal and that discussing feelings is a sign of strength, not weakness.

In fostering these open conversations, we help boys manage their current stress and anxiety and equip them with the emotional tools they'll need to handle future challenges. By recognizing the signs, employing effective management techniques, creating supportive environments, and encouraging open emotional communication, we lay down a foundation of resilience and understanding that supports their emotional development into adolescence and beyond. As we continue exploring strategies for overcoming common challenges, remember that each step taken is building stronger, more emotionally intelligent young individuals ready to face the world with confidence and clarity.

5.4 Combating Stereotypes: Encouraging Healthy Expression

Boys today often feel pressured by narrow ideas of masculinity, limiting their freedom to express themselves fully. To break these stereotypes, it's vital to create environments at home and in school where emotional expression is encouraged for everyone. Boys need to know that emotions like empathy, sadness, and fear are universal, not tied to gender. Exposing them to diverse stories and media featuring men in various roles broadens their emotional range and interests. Emphasizing diversity teaches boys the value of different cultures and resilience in handling emotions. Teaching media literacy helps them question stereotypes and see emotional openness as a strength. Supporting boys in exploring their interests, whether in dance, cooking, engineering, or sports, without societal judgment, validates their choices and promotes their personal growth. This approach not only benefits boys but also pushes society toward greater emotional understanding and inclusivity.

5.5 Building Confidence Through Self-Awareness

Self-awareness is about tuning in to our feelings, thoughts, and actions. For boys, it's recognizing what excites them, what brings them down, and why they react as they do in different situations. This awareness can change how they tackle challenges, moving from reactive to proactive. For example, if a boy knows he gets stressed before a test, he can use strategies like talking about his worries or using relaxation techniques. Imagine a boy at a diving board, toes over the edge, heart racing. It's more than just a jump; it's a lesson in self-awareness and confidence. As he leaps, he discovers not just his physical abilities but also his courage. Fostering self-awareness empowers boys to face challenges confidently, shaping a promising future.

Activities to Boost Self-Awareness

Let's dive into enjoyable activities that boost self-awareness. Journaling is a timeless tool; encourage boys to jot down daily experiences and emotions, helping them recognize and name feelings. Combine this with mindfulness practices, such as simple breathing exercises or child-friendly apps, to teach boys to stay present and attentive, fostering non-judgmental self-awareness.Mindfulness can also involve listening and speaking exercises, teaching boys to focus fully on conversations without planning responses, enhancing self-awareness. Engaging them in personal challenges, like learning new skills or hobbies, offers tangible evidence of growth, boosting both self-awareness and confidence.

Setting Achievable Goals

Setting goals is essential for personal growth. Start small to ensure success; for example, if a boy loves basketball, he might aim to practice shooting for fifteen minutes daily. Achieving these goals boosts confidence, encouraging them to set more challenging ones, like joining a school basketball team. Reflecting on and celebrating these wins reinforces their self-awareness and abilities.

Integrating goal-setting sessions into routines provides structured opportunities for boys to plan their achievements. These sessions foster discussions on resilience and self-awareness, reinforcing the connection between effort and outcomes.

Learning from Role Models

Role models are pivotal in how boys perceive and develop confidence through self-awareness. Sharing stories of individuals who demonstrate self-awareness and confidence in their personal and professional lives can inspire boys to foster these qualities in themselves. For instance, athletes often speak about the role of mental preparation and self-awareness in their performance. Interviews or biographies of such individuals can highlight how understanding their strengths, weaknesses, and emotional states has played a crucial role in their successes and how they've used setbacks as learning opportunities. This reassures parents, educators, and caregivers that their efforts in fostering self-awareness and emotional intelligence are supported by external influences, making the journey less daunting and more rewarding.

Involving guest speakers and hosting interactive sessions with role models from diverse sectors offers boys tangible examples of how self-awareness fuels confidence and success. This approach makes learning active and stimulating by allowing boys to engage directly, pose queries, and glean insights from others' journeys. It underscores the ongoing nature of developing self-awareness and confidence, motivating boys to strive towards genuine self-expression and understanding.

By integrating these strategies—activities that boost self-awareness, structured goal-setting, and learning from role models—we equip boys with the tools to understand themselves better and, consequently, to interact with the world with greater confidence. This understanding allows them to navigate their paths with clarity and assurance, ready to tackle challenges head-on and thrive in diverse situations. As we explore these strategies, remember that each step to enhance self-awareness builds confidence and lays a foundation for lifelong emotional intelligence and personal fulfillment.

5.6 Emotional Intelligence in Conflict Resolution

Imagine two young boys in a heated debate over whose turn it is to use the playground slide. Voices rise, gestures become animated, and the situation teeters on the edge of turning from verbal disagreement to physical confrontation. This scene, common in playgrounds, classrooms, and even homes, underscores the importance of teaching boys effective conflict resolution from a young age. Conflict resolution isn't just about stopping fights; it's about equipping boys with the skills to handle disagreements in ways that strengthen relationships rather than strain them. It's about turning conflicts into opportunities for growth and understanding.

Understanding Conflict Resolution

Conflict resolution involves identifying and addressing disagreements in a manner that is respectful and constructive to all parties involved. It requires a set of skills essential for maintaining healthy interpersonal relationships and for fostering a supportive community. When boys learn to resolve conflicts effectively, they not only navigate their current social landscapes more smoothly but also lay the groundwork for healthier interactions in their future personal and professional lives. Effective conflict resolution contributes to a boy's emotional intelligence by enhancing his ability to understand his emotions and those of others, communicate effectively, and negotiate solutions that respect everyone's needs.

Strategies for Peaceful Resolution

Teaching boys strategies for peaceful conflict resolution begins with active listening. Active listening involves fully concentrating on what is being said rather than passively hearing the speaker's message. It includes listening with all senses and giving full attention to the speaker. Guide boys to practice this by paraphrasing what the other person has said before responding, showing that they truly understand the other's perspective. Another key strategy is the use of *"I" statements*. Teach them to frame their responses regarding how they feel rather than what the other person has done wrong, for example, **"I feel upset when I'm interrupted"** instead of **"You're always talking over me."** This approach decreases defensiveness, opening up space for more empathetic interactions.

Finding a compromise also plays a crucial role in resolving conflicts. It involves both parties working together to find a mutually acceptable solution. This might mean taking turns, sharing resources, or even coming up with a completely new solution that neither had considered. Encouraging boys to think creatively about how everyone's needs can be met can transform a conflict from a win-lose situation to a win-win scenario.

Role-Playing Conflict Scenarios

For younger boys, role-playing, as previously discussed, is one effective way to practice these skills in a controlled, supportive environment. By acting out common conflicts and working through them using the strategies discussed, boys can gain confidence in their ability to handle disputes constructively. For instance, setting up a role-play scenario where one boy wants to play soccer and another wants to play basketball could allow them to explore various solutions, practice active listening, use "I" statements, and negotiate a compromise. This hands-on practice makes the abstract principles of conflict resolution concrete and applicable in everyday situations.

The Role of Empathy in Conflict Resolution

Empathy is at the heart of effective conflict resolution. It allows boys to understand and share another person's feelings, providing a foundation for more compassionate and effective interactions. When boys learn to view situations from another's perspective, they are more likely to engage in fair and peaceful resolutions. Empathy fosters forgiveness and reduces the likelihood of conflicts leading to resentment or bitterness. By emphasizing empathy in every step of conflict resolution—from listening and expressing feelings to finding compromises—you nurture boys' ability to connect with others on a deeper level, enhancing their relationships and overall emotional well-being.

Integrating these elements of conflict resolution into boys' everyday experiences prepares them to deal with disagreements and enhances their emotional intelligence, equipping them with life skills. It transforms potential conflicts into opportunities for learning and connection, promoting a more empathetic, understanding approach to differences. As we wrap up this exploration of emotional intelligence in conflict resolution, we set the stage for nurturing more competent communicators and more compassionate individuals, ready to build and sustain positive relationships in all areas of their lives.

CHAPTER HIGHLIGHTS & ACTION POINTS:

- Navigating Peer Pressure:

    - Peer pressure isn't just about dares; it's about influencing choices and values.

    - Equip boys with assertive communication and role-playing.

    - Encourage friendships with shared values and interests.

- Anger Management:

    - Help boys identify what sets off their anger and express it healthily.

    - Teach techniques like deep breathing and journaling.

    - Show how adults handle anger constructively.

- Stress Management:

    - Be attentive to signs of stress and anxiety, and encourage open conversations.

    - Introduce mindfulness and create calm environments.

    - Foster a safe space for boys to express their feelings.

- Breaking Stereotypes:

    - Emphasize the importance of diverse emotional expression.

    - Expose boys to varied media and role models.

    - Encourage exploration without societal judgment.

- Confidence Building:

    - Help boys recognize their strengths and weaknesses.

    - Set achievable goals and celebrate successes.

    - Share stories of individuals who demonstrate self-awareness and confidence.

- Conflict Resolution:

    - Teach boys to resolve disagreements respectfully.

    - Practice active listening and empathy.

    - Act out conflicts to practice resolution skills.

Chapter Six

Communication and Connection

Imagine a scene at a bustling family reunion where a young boy tries to tell his grandfather about his latest soccer game. Amid the laughter and chatter, his story gets lost, and his excitement fades into a quiet resignation. This moment, although small, highlights the critical nature of communication and, mainly, the power of listening. In this chapter, we focus on nurturing deeper connections with boys through effective communication, starting with the cornerstone of all great relationships: active listening.

6.1 Active Listening: Connecting with Your Boy

Principles of Active Listening

Active listening is more than just hearing words; it's about engagement and understanding. It involves giving your full attention to the speaker, reflecting on what's said, and withholding judgment. Let's break this down: giving full attention means putting aside distractions, whether it's your phone, the dinner you're cooking, or the thoughts of your next work task. Reflecting content is about mirroring back what you've heard, not just to show you were listening but to ensure you've understood correctly. Withholding judgment is the trickiest; it means keeping an open mind, allowing the boy to express his thoughts and feelings without fear of immediate criticism or advice.

Practicing Active Listening with Boys

Active listening can transform your interactions with boys, creating a space where they feel valued and understood. Start by getting down to their eye level. This simple physical gesture can make a big difference in how connected they feel during the conversation. Maintain eye contact and use nods or simple affirmatives to show you're engaged. When they finish, summarize what you've heard before responding with your thoughts or advice. This practice validates their feelings and helps them develop trust, knowing their words genuinely matter to you.

Active Listening in Conflict

In moments of conflict, active listening becomes even more crucial. It can defuse tension and lead to a quicker, more amicable resolution. When a boy is upset or angry, listen first without interrupting. Often, the act of expressing feelings aloud can help lower emotional intensity. After he's shared, reflect on the emotions you've heard, for example, "It sounds like you're really upset because your sister broke your model airplane." This reflection helps him understand that you grasp the depth of his feelings, which can be soothing.

Activities to Enhance Listening Skills

Engaging in interactive activities can be fun and educational to strengthen listening skills. Storytelling is a fantastic way to practice. You could start a story and ask him to finish it, focusing on recalling details accurately, which hones his ability to listen and remember. Listening games like '**Simon Says**' or '**I Spy**' are also great, especially for younger boys, as they require careful listening to succeed. For something more advanced, try '**Two Truths and a Lie**', which tests listening and critical thinking as he discerns which statements are true.

Interactive Element: Listening Journal

Consider introducing a listening journal. After practicing active listening, you and the boy can jot down what you learned about each other that day. This can be an eye-opening exercise, revealing just how much can be learned through careful listening. It can also serve as a great way to track the improvement in your communication over time. For much younger boys, instead of journaling, simple conversation to reflect on what was learned from each other will do.

In embracing these practices, you create a foundation for better understanding and deeper connections that foster trust and openness. As we continue to explore the dynamics of communication and connection, remember that at the heart of all great relationships is the ability to truly listen to one another.

6.2 Encouraging Boys to Share Their Feelings

Creating a space where boys feel safe to share their emotions is vital. It's like tending to a garden; it requires patience, the right environment, and careful nurturing. You can foster this environment by carving out specific spots in your home or classroom where open dialogue is encouraged—a cozy corner with comfy seating for privacy or uninterrupted car rides. Consistency in these judgment-free zones is crucial, ensuring that every emotion receives support and understanding, not criticism or immediate solutions.

Boys often hesitate to share their feelings due to fear of judgment or a lack of words to describe complex emotions. Society often sends the message that vulnerability isn't 'manly.' To counter this, affirm their feelings when they express them, reinforcing that all emotions are valid and it's okay to struggle finding the right words. Encourage them to express themselves in their own way without interruption or correction. This validation encourages them to explore and express their emotions confidently.

Art and play can be powerful tools for helping boys express emotions they may not yet understand fully. Art offers a visual and tactile way to convey feelings, where colors and shapes can represent internal states. Consider regular art sessions where the focus is on the process, not the end result, asking questions like, "How did you feel while creating this?" Similarly, play, especially role-playing, allows boys to project their feelings onto characters, giving them a safe space to explore complex emotions. These activities provide a release and gradually expand their emotional understanding.

Daily Emotional Check-Ins

Introduce a daily routine of emotional check-ins. It could be a relaxed chat over dinner or a few minutes before bedtime where you ask about the highs and lows of their day. The key is to listen actively without jumping in to solve problems. These moments are for understanding and sharing, not fixing everything. For younger boys, a 'feelings chart' with faces showing different emotions can be helpful. They can point to how they felt throughout the day, making it easier for them to express their feelings.

By consistently providing safe spaces, validating emotions, using creative expressions, and having regular emotional check-ins, you create a nurturing environment that encourages boys to share and process their feelings. This approach not only opens up lines of communication but also fosters deeper connections and emotional intelligence, setting the foundation for healthier emotional expression as they grow.

6.3 The Art of Empathetic Conversation

Empathy is crucial for communication. It's more than just sharing feelings; it's about really connecting and building trust. Try weaving empathy into everyday moments. When your son is upset about losing a soccer game, instead of jumping in with advice or brushing off his feelings, just acknowledge his disappointment and try to understand his perspective. This kind of support helps him process his emotions and feel validated.

Teaching empathy also means setting an example. Kids, especially boys, learn a lot by watching us. If they see us being compassionate and understanding, they're more likely to do the same. Be mindful of how you talk about feelings, handle conflicts, and even engage in daily conversations. For instance, when you're dealing with a sensitive issue with a family member, let your son see you using kind words and considering the other person's feelings. These everyday actions show him how empathy can improve communication and relationships.

When you're looking to foster empathy during conversations with boys, consider using open-ended questions that encourage them to think about and express their feelings. Questions like, **"How did that experience make you feel?"** or **"What do you think your friend felt when that happened?"** prompt deeper reflection and understanding. These questions help develop their emotional vocabulary and encourage them to consider the perspectives and feelings of others, which is a cornerstone of empathetic engagement.

Non-verbal cues are crucial for showing empathy. Simple gestures like making eye contact, nodding, and having an open posture show you're really listening and care. When your son talks about something important, leaning in and maintaining eye contact makes him feel heard and valued. A gentle touch, like a hand on his shoulder, can provide comfort, especially during tough times. These small actions can significantly enhance his sense of support and connection.

Interactive Element: Empathy Role-Playing Cards

To help your son develop empathetic communication skills, try using empathy role-playing cards. Each card can describe a situation, like a friend losing a pet, a sibling failing a test, or a parent stressed about work. By acting out these scenarios, he can practice responding with compassion and learn to apply empathy in different contexts. This makes learning about empathy fun and engaging, deepening his understanding of how to use it in real-life interactions.

Through these discussions and practices, we can master empathetic conversation, turning every interaction into an opportunity to connect deeply and build stronger relationships. Remember, empathy is a gift that enriches both the giver and the receiver, enhancing every conversation and deepening every relationship.

6.4 Setting Boundaries with Love and Respect

In relationships, boundaries are essential for emotional well-being and forming healthy connections. For young boys, learning about boundaries is crucial for respecting themselves and others. Teaching boys about boundaries is like giving them a map for navigating relationships. It guides them on when to say yes, how to say no, and how to respect others' limits.

Explain that boundaries are personal rules for how others should treat them and how they will respond if those rules are broken. Boys need to know they can say no if they're uncomfortable, whether it's an unwanted hug or peer pressure. Use scenarios like **"What would you do if a friend wanted to copy your homework?"** or **"How would you tell someone you don't like being tickled?"** to help them understand and articulate their feelings.

Role-play conversations to teach boys how to assert their limits respectfully, using phrases like **"I'm not comfortable with that"** or **"I'd prefer to do this instead."** Reinforce that setting boundaries is about self-care and respect, not confrontation. Praise them when they handle situations well to reinforce these behaviors.

Respecting others' boundaries is equally important. Teach boys to notice verbal cues and body language and to ask permission before entering personal spaces or borrowing items. Encourage them to accept 'no' without argument, building empathy and respect.

Balancing boundaries with connection is key. Encourage boys to express their needs without severing ties, like saying, **"I need some quiet time right now, but can we talk/play later?"** Regular family discussions about feelings and boundaries can normalize these conversations and strengthen bonds. By integrating these practices, boys learn to protect their space, respect others, and maintain healthy relationships, growing into men who value love and respect through healthy boundaries.

6.5 The Role of Family Rituals in Emotional Bonding

Imagine the warmth and laughter of a family gathering around the dinner table, sharing stories from their day—this simple daily ritual, often taken for granted, is a powerful tool for strengthening family bonds and providing a sense of security and belonging. Family rituals, whether they are daily meals together, bedtime stories, or weekend hikes, serve as anchors in the bustling flow of life. They offer predictable structure and comfort, especially for boys navigating the challenges of growing up. These moments are not just about what is done but how it is done— they are imbued with shared meanings and values, reinforcing family unity and providing a sense of identity.

Building emotional bonds through rituals starts with recognizing their power to connect. Regular family meals, for instance, are not just about nourishment for the body but also for relationships. They offer a dedicated time to reconnect, discuss the highs and lows of the day, and listen to each other's experiences and feelings. This daily gathering becomes a ritual that boys can rely on for consistency and comfort, knowing that no matter how tough the day, the family will come together in the evening. Similarly, bedtime stories, a favorite ritual for many families, are a time for closeness and sharing. The stories told can convey values, spark imagination, and provide a soothing transition to sleep, all while reinforcing the bond between parent and child.

Encouraging families to create their own rituals that reflect their unique values and interests can further enhance these connections. Perhaps your family loves the outdoors—establishing a ritual of weekend nature walks can be a wonderful way to cultivate a shared love for nature while spending quality time together. Or maybe creativity is a central value in your home; setting aside time each week for a family art project can allow everyone to express themselves and appreciate each other's creativity. The key is to choose activities that resonate with the interests of the family members, making these rituals eagerly anticipated events that everyone enjoys.

Rituals also significantly mark special occasions such as birthdays, holidays, and other milestones. These are opportunities to celebrate individual and family achievements, to honor traditions, and to make lasting memories. Birthday rituals might include a special meal chosen by the birthday boy, a family game night, or a storytelling session where family members share funny or touching stories about the person celebrating their birthday. Holiday rituals, whether decorating the house together, preparing a special meal, or volunteering at a community center, imbue these times with deeper meaning and closeness. These special occasion rituals make the day memorable and reinforce the values and bonds that hold the family together.

Addressing more sad times, family rituals can provide comfort and a sense of continuity during periods of loss or change. When a family faces the loss of a loved one, rituals can help in the grieving process. This might include gathering to share stories about the person, visiting their favorite places, or participating in activities they loved. These rituals help honor the memory of the loved one while providing a structured way to express grief and support each other. They serve as a reminder that while someone may be gone, the family remains, continuing to support and cherish each other in the face of loss. Additionally, rituals can help boys manage transitions such as moving to a new city or adjusting to their parent's divorce. Rituals that remain constant despite the change—like the continued bedtime story or Sunday morning pancakes—can provide a reassuring sense of normalcy and security.

In weaving these rituals into the fabric of family life, you not only strengthen the emotional bonds between family members but also create a shared history that provides comfort and joy throughout life. These rituals become the memories boys will cherish into adulthood, the stories they will share with their children, continuing the legacy of closeness, resilience, and familial love. So, whether through daily routines, celebrations of special occasions, or rituals that bring comfort in times of change, remember that these shared moments are the threads that bind the family together, crafting a tapestry of connection that lasts a lifetime.

6.6 Nurturing Emotional Intelligence in Sibling Relationships

Sibling relationships are among the earliest and most influential social interactions in a boy's life. These relationships can significantly shape emotional intelligence and teaching skills, from sharing and cooperation to empathy and conflict resolution. Sibling dynamics are unique in that they blend familial love with peer-like competition and camaraderie, creating a complex but rich ground for emotional growth.

Understanding the impact of these relationships on emotional development is crucial. Siblings often practice their first negotiations, share profound life changes, and develop deep emotional bonds with each other. These interactions can enhance social understanding and emotional regulation as siblings learn to navigate each other's moods and preferences. However, these relationships can also be a source of rivalry and conflict, presenting opportunities for boys to learn conflict resolution and empathy in a safe environment. The key is guiding them to view these challenges as chances to strengthen bonds rather than as threats.

Fostering empathy among siblings is crucial for their emotional intelligence development. Model empathetic behavior to encourage siblings to emulate it and promote understanding by engaging them in cooperative activities and regular family meetings where everyone shares their thoughts and feelings. This nurtures mutual respect and deeper connections. Addressing sibling conflicts with emotional intelligence is key. Instead of merely resolving disputes, use these moments as opportunities to teach valuable lessons in interpersonal skills and self-awareness. Encourage using "I" statements to express feelings and needs, such as **"I feel upset when you borrow my things without asking."** Facilitate listening exercises and role-play conflict scenarios to help them understand each other's perspectives and find mutually satisfying solutions. Celebrating each other's achievements is vital for strengthening sibling bonds and fostering a supportive family environment. Encourage siblings to cheer for one another, recognize accomplishments, and celebrate personal milestones. Introduce a **"brag board"** in the home for siblings to post notes about each other's successes, reinforcing a culture of support and collective achievement.

As siblings mature, the emotional competencies developed through sibling interactions—empathy, understanding, and conflict resolution—are crucial building blocks for strong, lasting friendships and professional relationships. Navigating the nuances of sibling dynamics with emotional intelligence fosters individual growth and enhances family cohesion. These foundational experiences with siblings pave the way for broader social skills that are instrumental throughout life. Encouraging empathy, teaching conflict resolution, and celebrating successes fortify sibling bonds and set the stage for fulfilling relationships in all spheres of life. As we proceed, we'll delve into fostering resilience and independence, strengthening the emotional foundation crucial for life's challenges and triumphs.

CHAPTER HIGHLIGHTS & ACTION POINTS:

- Active Listening:

  - Key principles: full attention, reflecting content, withholding judgment.

  - Techniques include eye contact, summarizing, and validating feelings.

- Encouraging Emotional Expression:

  - Create safe spaces for boys to share feelings without fear.

  - Utilize art, play, and daily emotional check-ins.

  - Make daily emotional check-ins a routine.

- Empathetic Conversation:

  - Use open-ended questions and set examples of empathy.

  - Non-verbal cues like eye contact enhance connection.

  - Use role-playing cards and discussions to build empathy.

- Setting and Respecting Boundaries:

  - Teach boys to assert boundaries respectfully.

  - Balance assertiveness with maintaining connections.

  - Role-play boundary-setting scenarios and praise respectful behavior.

- Family Rituals for Bonding:

- Daily and special rituals strengthen family bonds.

- Create unique rituals reflecting shared values.

- Nurturing Sibling Relationships:

  - Foster empathy and conflict resolution among siblings.

  - Celebrate achievements and encourage cooperation.

Chapter Seven

Emotional Intelligence in School and Social Settings

Imagine a classroom where laughter and learning go hand in hand—a place where each student not only thrives academically but also grows emotionally. This isn't just a hopeful vision; it's a feasible reality when emotional intelligence is woven into the fabric of educational environments. In this chapter, we dive into how schools and educators can foster emotional intelligence (EI) in the classroom, transforming traditional learning spaces into nurturing grounds for intellectual and emotional development.

7.1 Emotional Intelligence in the Classroom

Integrating Emotional Learning

Integrating emotional intelligence into daily classroom activities isn't about adding more to your plate as an educator or parent; it's about infusing what you already do with an awareness of emotions. Start with the curriculum—literature classes offer fertile ground for discussing characters' emotional responses and motivations, providing a natural context for students to explore and relate these emotions to their own experiences. In science or social studies, discussing the emotional impact of historical events or scientific discoveries can add depth and relevance to the facts.

Math might seem less intuitive for emotional integration, but consider the anxiety or frustration students often feel in this subject. Addressing these emotions openly can transform students' approach to problem-solving. For example, before starting a math lesson, you might have a brief discussion about feelings toward the subject and share strategies for managing frustration or anxiety. This simple acknowledgment can relieve tension and foster a more supportive learning environment.

Interactive elements like emotional check-ins can also enhance EI integration. Starting the day with a quick round where students share how they feel can help them become more aware of their emotions and build empathy and connection among classmates. This practice encourages students to recognize and respect diverse emotional experiences, fostering a classroom culture of empathy and support.

Teacher-Student Relationships

The relationships between teachers and students are pivotal in shaping the classroom's emotional climate. As an educator, your emotional intelligence directly influences your students' emotional and academic success. When you model empathy, active listening, and genuine concern for your students' emotional well-being, you create a safe space where students feel valued and understood. This supportive environment encourages risk-taking and resilience, which are essential for intellectual growth and emotional development.

Consider the power of personalized feedback—when giving feedback on assignments, focus not only on the academic aspects but also on the student's effort and emotional journey. This approach shows that you value their learning process, enhancing their motivation and engagement.

Peer Mediation Programs

Peer mediation programs are vital in teaching conflict resolution and empathy, which are central to emotional intelligence. These initiatives equip students with the tools to amicably resolve conflicts and appreciate diverse perspectives, benefiting both individual participants and the wider school community through reduced conflict and increased empathy. Starting with a small group of trained upper-grade students can set the stage for broader cultural change within the school, embedding empathy and understanding as core values of the school's ethos.

Emotional Intelligence and Academic Success

The link between emotional intelligence and academic success is well-documented. Students with high EI tend to have better focus, more motivation, and stronger resilience—all key components of academic success. They are better equipped to handle the stresses of school life, from test anxiety to peer relationships, and they often show enhanced problem-solving abilities.

To foster this, consider incorporating group projects that require emotional skills like cooperation, perspective-taking, and leadership. These projects can help students apply emotional intelligence in real-world scenarios, reinforcing the connection between their emotional skills and academic performance.

By integrating emotional intelligence into classroom dynamics, enhancing teacher-student relationships, implementing peer mediation, and linking EI to academic success, educators and parents can create an educational experience that nurtures the mind and heart. This holistic approach to education prepares students for academic challenges. It equips them with the emotional skills necessary to thrive beyond school.

7.2 Bullying: An Emotional Intelligence Response

Understanding Bullying from an EI Perspective

Bullying is not just a series of isolated incidents or a simple clash of personalities. It's a complex social dynamic that profoundly affects the emotional climate of any environment, especially schools. Through the lens of emotional intelligence (EI), bullying can be seen as a breakdown of understanding and empathy among students. It often stems from a lack of emotional regulation and an inability to recognize and respect the feelings of others. When a child engages in bullying, it might be a misguided attempt at expressing their own unresolved feelings of anger, frustration, or insecurity. Conversely, victims of bullying often experience feelings of helplessness, fear, and sadness, which can lead to severe emotional and academic repercussions if not addressed.

To tackle bullying effectively, it's crucial to understand its emotional underpinnings. For instance, a bully might be struggling with issues at home and is using aggression as a coping mechanism. This doesn't excuse the behavior but helps address the root cause rather than merely the symptoms. Similarly, empowering victims involves more than just teaching them how to stand up for themselves; it's about helping them rebuild their self-esteem and trust in their ability to forge respectful relationships. Recognizing these emotional currents can guide more effective interventions that stop the immediate bullying and heal the underlying emotional wounds.

Empowerment Through Emotional Skills

Empowering both victims and bystanders of bullying with emotional intelligence skills is key to transforming the school environment from one of passive observation to active support and respect. Teaching emotional self-awareness allows victims to articulate their feelings and understand their emotional responses are valid and important. This self-awareness also helps them recognize the impact of bullying on their emotions and behaviors, equipping them with the knowledge to seek help and express their needs clearly.

On the other hand, bystanders can be taught to use empathy and social responsibility to intervene effectively. Many students don't intervene in bullying situations, not because they agree with the behavior, but because they may not know how to or fear becoming targets themselves. By fostering a strong sense of empathy and collective responsibility, bystanders can be encouraged to support their peers, whether by speaking out, reporting the behavior, or simply offering their presence as a form of solidarity with the victim.

Role of School Culture

The overall culture of a school plays a pivotal role in deterring or perpetuating bullying. A culture that celebrates diversity, practices inclusivity, and promotes a deep understanding of emotional intelligence creates a safe space for all students. This environment implicitly discourages bullying by fostering respect and empathy among students and staff. Creating such a culture involves consistent efforts from everyone in the school community to model and reinforce these values.

School leaders and teachers can set the tone by openly discussing the importance of emotional intelligence in assemblies, classrooms, and staff meetings. Celebrating acts of kindness, empathy, and academic achievements can reinforce the value placed on emotional intelligence. Furthermore, integrating emotional education into the curriculum and everyday interactions helps normalize discussions about emotions, making it easier for students to express themselves and recognize the emotional needs of their peers.

Restorative Practices

Restorative practices offer a powerful alternative to traditional disciplinary actions, which often focus more on punishment than on healing. These practices involve open dialogues facilitated by an unbiased mediator, where all parties involved in the bullying incident come together to discuss the impact of their actions and work collectively towards a resolution. This approach not only holds the bully accountable constructively but also gives the victim a voice in their advocacy. It emphasizes healing the relationships and restoring the emotional balance rather than inflicting punitive measures.

Implementing restorative practices requires careful planning and sensitivity. It involves training staff to handle these meetings empathetically and fairly, ensuring every student's emotional perspective is heard and validated. These meetings can also provide valuable insights into the student body's emotional dynamics, offering further opportunities for promoting emotional intelligence throughout the school.

By addressing bullying with emotional intelligence, schools can create environments that nurture respect, empathy, and understanding among students. This approach not only combats bullying but also builds a foundation of emotional skills that students will carry into all areas of their lives, promoting healthier relationships and a more empathetic society.

7.3 Building Supportive Friendships

Friendships are a cornerstone of young boys' emotional growth and well-being, offering a primary source of companionship, learning, and support. When boys understand what makes a friendship healthy and supportive, it can significantly impact how they interact with their peers and how they see themselves in these relationships.

A supportive friendship is built on mutual respect, trust, empathy, and understanding. In such relationships, both friends feel valued and supported, comfortable sharing their thoughts and feelings without fear of judgment. There's a healthy balance of give and take, with both parties contributing equally to the relationship.

Helping boys develop and nurture friendships with emotional intelligence is vital. Encouraging participation in sports, arts, or science clubs can help them connect with like-minded peers, creating a solid foundation for friendship. It's also important to teach boys to listen and show genuine interest in others' feelings and experiences. Asking open-ended questions like, **"What did you enjoy about your weekend?"** or **"What do you think about our current class book?"** can deepen these budding relationships.

Maintaining friendships requires effort and care. Boys need to understand the importance of consistent communication through regular playdates, sharing meals at school, or routine check-ins. It's equally crucial for them to learn how to handle conflicts constructively. Teaching boys to express their feelings openly and respectfully, and the importance of apology and forgiveness, can strengthen friendships against the inevitable challenges. Role-playing different social situations, from misunderstandings to disagreements, can help boys practice handling real-life interactions with more skill.

Challenges in friendships, like jealousy, peer pressure, and conflicts, are common and need to be managed well. Boys can learn to recognize jealousy in themselves or their friends and address these feelings openly and sensitively. For instance, if a boy feels jealous of a friend's achievements in sports, discussing these feelings can prevent resentment. Similarly, understanding how to resist peer pressure by staying true to one's values and beliefs can help maintain integrity and healthy friendships. Techniques like assertiveness training, where boys practice saying no confidently, can be very helpful.

Parents and caregivers play a crucial role in guiding boys through the complexities of friendships. By modeling healthy relationships and emotional intelligence in their interactions, adults set a powerful example for boys. Parents can facilitate social interactions, supervise playdates to ensure positive experiences, and discuss any concerns that arise. Encouraging conversations about the day's social interactions gives boys a safe space to process their feelings and develop strategies for handling different social situations. After a playdate, a parent might ask, **"What was the most fun part of today, and was there anything that bothered you?"** This encourages boys to reflect on their interactions and better understand their own social and emotional responses.

By creating an environment where emotional intelligence is regularly discussed and practiced, parents and educators can help boys build and maintain friendships that enrich their lives and support their emotional development. These friendships, grounded in mutual respect and understanding, enhance their current well-being and lay the groundwork for healthy interpersonal relationships in the future. Through these efforts, boys learn to navigate the complexities of human relationships with empathy, respect, and emotional insight, growing into emotionally intelligent individuals who value and contribute positively to their relationships.

7.4 Group Activities That Foster Teamwork and Empathy

Imagine the buzz of excitement and the flurry of activity as a group of boys work together to build the tallest tower possible using only spaghetti and marshmallows. This scene isn't just about fun and games; it's a carefully designed team-building exercise that promotes skills like cooperation, communication, and problem-solving, all underpinned by a foundation of empathy. Such activities are engaging and immensely valuable in teaching boys how to work with others, understand different perspectives, and contribute to a common goal. Here, we'll explore a variety of team-building exercises and delve into how they can enhance empathy and cooperation among peers.

Team-building exercises are a fantastic way to break down barriers and build connections between students. These activities require each member to contribute their unique strengths and to rely on others to achieve a common goal, mirroring the collaborative nature of real-world projects and relationships. For instance, a challenge like a treasure hunt not only demands physical activity but also needs strategic thinking and effective communication. Each participant might naturally take on roles that require empathy—considering what others might not see or expressing what needs to be communicated more clearly. Activities like these make the abstract concept of teamwork tangible and make learning these skills enjoyable and memorable.

Another powerful team-building activity is the **'problem-solving relay,'** in which groups are faced with a series of challenges that they must solve within a time limit. Each challenge could be tailored to involve different emotional intelligence components, such as interpreting nonverbal cues or managing group emotions during stressful tasks. This fosters a sense of urgency and excitement and encourages boys to work under pressure while maintaining empathy and respect for each other's ideas and feelings.

Community Service Projects

Community service projects significantly broaden boys' horizons, instilling empathy and social responsibility. By participating in activities such as visiting local nursing homes, boys gain unique insights into the lives of older people, enriching their understanding of diversity and history. Environmental clean-up initiatives teach the value of individual and collective action in preserving our planet and fostering teamwork toward a sustainable future. These experiences emphasize the importance of empathy, community engagement, and environmental stewardship, encouraging boys to appreciate the broader impact of their actions.

Inclusive Group Dynamics

Ensuring that group activities are inclusive is crucial in allowing every boy to contribute and feel valued. This can be facilitated by consciously designing activities that require diverse skills and abilities, ensuring that every participant can shine in some way. For instance, while some boys may excel in physical tasks, others might thrive in roles that require thoughtful planning or creative thinking. By rotating roles and responsibilities in group activities, you give each boy a chance to lead and contribute, reinforcing their sense of worth and belonging.

It's also important to be vigilant about group dynamics to ensure that no one is consistently sidelined or overshadowed by more dominant personalities. This might involve setting clear guidelines about turn-taking or using random methods to choose group leaders or spokespersons, thus giving each boy a fair chance to lead and influence the group's decisions. These practices promote fairness and teach boys the value of democracy and respect for others' opinions, which are essential components of empathy.

Learning from Group Successes and Failures

Group activities serve as a prime learning environment, where celebrating triumphs boosts confidence and teamwork, and analyzing setbacks offers invaluable lessons in resilience and problem-solving. Debriefing post-activity is pivotal for boys to perceive challenges not as barriers but as avenues for growth. For instance, after a team project, facilitating a discussion on effective strategies and areas for improvement fosters an environment where constructive feedback is valued, and failures are seen as opportunities for emotional and resilience development. This nurtures continuous learning and adaptability, key traits for success in all life's arenas. Incorporating team-building tasks, community service, inclusive practices, and reflective learning equips boys with empathy, cooperation, and social responsibility skills. These activities prepare them for academic teamwork and lifelong, empathetic collaboration in diverse communities.

7.5 The Role of Teachers and Coaches

Teachers and coaches play vital roles far beyond their traditional duties in the bustling hallways of schools and the dynamic sidelines of sports fields. They're not just educators and mentors but also significant emotional anchors in the lives of young boys. Their ability to model emotional intelligence (EI) sets a tone that can significantly influence a boy's ability to manage his emotions and interact harmoniously with others. When a teacher or coach consistently demonstrates empathy, patience, and emotional awareness, it sends a powerful message: **that understanding and managing one's emotions are as crucial as academic knowledge or athletic skill.**

Consider the impact of a coach who, after a tough loss, focuses not only on what went wrong but also on how the team feels. By opening a discussion about disappointment and strategies for emotional recovery, the coach is doing more than soothing bruised egos; he is teaching resilience. Similarly, a teacher who notices a student's frustration with a difficult task and takes the time to talk through the student's feelings is providing a lesson in emotional regulation that is likely to resonate far beyond the classroom.

Emotional Support in Education and Sports

Emotional support is a cornerstone of effective teaching and coaching. It involves recognizing that each student or athlete is not just a learner or a player but a complex individual with emotions that can significantly impact their engagement and performance. Providing emotional support might involve a teacher creating a supportive classroom atmosphere where students feel safe to express confusion or anxiety without fear of ridicule. In sports, it might involve a coach recognizing the signs of stress or burnout and encouraging an athlete to take the necessary time to recuperate.

Promoting a growth mindset is another critical area where emotional support from teachers and coaches can play a transformative role. This concept, developed by psychologist Carol Dweck, **posits that dedication and hard work can develop abilities and intelligence**. For a boy struggling with self-doubt, a teacher's reassurance that intelligence is not fixed and that persistence will lead to improvement can be a game-changer. It shifts his perception from **"I can't do this"** to **"I can't do this yet."** Coaches can foster a similar mindset in sports by focusing on effort and improvement rather than wins and losses, thus promoting resilience and a long-term love for the game.

Feedback and Constructive Criticism

How feedback is framed and delivered can significantly impact how it is received and used. Effective feedback in educational and athletic contexts is about more than pointing out errors; it's about guiding improvement and encouraging personal growth. For example, a teacher might use the **"sandwich" method**, where constructive criticism is between positive comments. This could involve praising a student's effort, offering a specific suggestion for improvement, and then reiterating confidence in the student's ability to improve. This method makes the criticism easier to accept and keeps the student motivated.

In sports, feedback can be immediate and continuous. A coach could provide real-time feedback during practice, pointing out strengths and areas for improvement. This ongoing feedback helps athletes adjust their techniques and strategies promptly, fostering a continuous learning environment that values growth and adaptability.

Recognizing and Addressing Emotional Needs

Teachers and coaches must adeptly recognize boys' emotional needs, often revealed by behavioral or performance changes. Basic training in emotional and psychological principles can help them spot signs of distress, like withdrawal, aggression, or declining performance, enabling timely interventions. This might include discussing feelings with the boy, involving counselors, or adjusting expectations to alleviate stress. Fostering an emotionally supportive environment also means equipping boys with an emotional vocabulary and tools for appropriate expression. Initiating sessions where students or athletes share their feelings can normalize emotional expression and foster empathy within the group.

Teachers and coaches play crucial roles in shaping the emotional lives of boys by embodying and teaching emotional intelligence. Their influence extends beyond the confines of classrooms and sports fields, helping to cultivate emotionally aware, resilient, and empathetic individuals ready to face the world's challenges with emotional savvy and maturity. Through their daily interactions, they are not just educating but profoundly shaping the future one boy at a time.

7.6 Social Skills for the Modern World

In today's fast-paced digital era, how we communicate and connect continues to evolve, bringing both challenges and opportunities, especially for young boys growing up amidst these changes. Adapting to digital communication is more than just learning how to use new platforms; it involves understanding how to maintain genuine connections and develop social skills in often virtual environments.

The digital world offers incredible opportunities for learning and connecting. Platforms like educational apps and social media can provide interactive, engaging ways to develop new skills and meet people from diverse backgrounds. However, navigating these spaces requires a nuanced understanding of digital etiquette and the emotional impact of online interactions. Teaching boys how to interact respectfully online is crucial. This includes understanding the permanence of digital footprints, the importance of privacy settings, and how to communicate thoughtfully. For instance, discussing the tone of text messages and the implications of posting specific content on social media can help boys appreciate the real-world consequences of their digital actions.

Moreover, fostering empathy in digital communications is vital. Boys must learn that behind every screen is a real person with feelings. Encouraging them to pause and think about how their words could affect others can cultivate a more empathetic approach to online interactions. While digital skills are essential, the importance of face-to-face interactions cannot be overstated. Direct, in-person communication fosters a deeper emotional connection, helping boys develop non-verbal communication skills such as reading body language and facial expressions. These interactions are instrumental in developing empathy and emotional intelligence. Therefore, balancing screen time with personal interactions is crucial. Encouraging activities that require in-person engagement, like team sports, music bands, or drama clubs, can help boys develop these critical social skills. Additionally, family activities that encourage conversation, like shared meals without screens, can reinforce these skills in a familiar, comfortable setting.

Preparing boys for the social challenges of the modern world involves equipping them with strategies to navigate a landscape marked by diversity, inclusion, and global connectivity. This preparation goes beyond teaching tolerance; it fosters a genuine appreciation and curiosity about different cultures and perspectives. Integrating global awareness into their learning through stories, media, and interactions with people from different backgrounds can broaden their understanding of the world. This global perspective is crucial for personal development and preparing them for the interconnected world they will enter as adults.

The skills boys develop today—be they digital etiquette, empathy in online and face-to-face interactions, or navigating diversity—will help them build stronger, more meaningful relationships throughout their lives. By guiding them through these complexities with a focus on emotional intelligence, you are helping to shape their future relationships and their broader worldviews.

As we wrap up this exploration into the social skills needed for the modern world, we're reminded of the intricate balance between digital and personal interactions in developing well-rounded, emotionally intelligent individuals. These lessons are pivotal as we prepare boys not only for the personal challenges they will face but also for their roles in a wider, increasingly connected world. Moving forward, the focus will shift to preparing for the future, where these foundational skills will be put to test as boys grow into young men navigating an ever-evolving landscape.

CHAPTER HIGHLIGHTS & ACTION POINTS:

- Emotional Intelligence in the Classroom

  - Emotional intelligence (EI) integration enhances both academic and emotional growth.

  - Curriculum integration: Literature, history, and science discussions can explore emotional responses and motivations.

  - Emotional check-ins and open discussions foster a supportive classroom culture.

  - Teacher-student relationships built on empathy and genuine concern improve student outcomes.

- Bullying: An Emotional Intelligence Response

  - Bullying stems from emotional misunderstandings and lack of empathy.

  - Addressing bullying through EI helps tackle root causes and supports both victims and perpetrators.

  - Empower bystanders to act with empathy is crucial and support victims actively. Foster a school culture of inclusivity and empathy.

- Building Supportive Friendships

  - Boys need guidance in developing, nurturing, and maintaining friendships.

  - Handling conflicts constructively strengthens friendships.

  - Role-playing social situations can improve interaction

skills.

- Teach boys to listen and show interest in others' feelings.

- Group Activities That Foster Teamwork and Empathy

  - Team-building exercises promote cooperation, empathy, and problem-solving.

  - Activities like treasure hunts and problem-solving relays enhance teamwork and emotional skills.

  - Community service projects teach empathy and social responsibility.

  - Rotate roles in group activities to ensure inclusivity and every participant feels valued.

- The Role of Teachers and Coaches

  - Teachers and coaches model emotional intelligence, influencing boys' emotional and social development.

  - Use the "sandwich" method for constructive feedback that enhances personal growth.

  - Recognize and address emotional needs is key to effectively teach and coach.

- Social Skills for the Modern World

  - Digital communication skills are essential in the modern world.Encourage in-person activities to develop non-verbal communication skills.

  - Teach boys respectful online communication and digital footprint awareness.

Chapter Eight

Preparing for the Future

As we watch the leaves turn and feel the crisp bite of autumn air, it's a reminder of change—a natural, inevitable part of life. For teenagers, this season of change isn't just about the weather; it marks a profound transition from childhood to adulthood. This period is filled with growth and transformation, not just physically but emotionally and socially. It's a time when emotional intelligence becomes more critical than ever, acting as a compass to navigate the complex world of adolescence. Emotional intelligence, or EI, is the toolkit that not only helps teens manage their emotions and forge solid relationships but also empowers them to make thoughtful decisions, instilling a sense of hope and optimism as they step more independently into the world.

8.1 Emotional Intelligence for Teenagers: Preparing for the Transition

Navigating Adolescent Changes

The teenage years are a rollercoaster of emotions, thanks to hormonal changes, evolving relationships, and increased pressures from school and beyond. These years are often marked by a search for identity, a desire for independence, and an acute awareness of peers and societal expectations. Emotional intelligence is crucial here as it helps teens manage the whirlwind of their feelings, understand and empathize with others, and navigate the challenges of growing up with confidence and self-awareness. For instance, an emotionally intelligent teenager can recognize when they're feeling overwhelmed by schoolwork and take proactive steps to manage their stress by talking it out or organizing their time better.

Identity and Self-Understanding

During adolescence, the quest to answer the question "Who am I?" becomes central. Emotional intelligence supports this journey of self-discovery by enhancing self-awareness. This means understanding and labeling one's emotions accurately, recognizing one's strengths and limitations, and seeing how emotions affect thoughts and actions. This self-knowledge is empowering—it can boost confidence and pave the way for a strong, authentic sense of self. Activities like journaling can be particularly beneficial during this stage, providing a private space for self-reflection and exploration.

Peer Relationships and Peer Pressure

Peer relationships take on heightened significance during the teenage years. These relationships are important not just for social enjoyment but also for developing social skills and identity. However, the desire to fit in can lead to peer pressure, which can challenge a teen's ability to stay true to themselves. Emotional intelligence provides the skills needed to navigate these dynamics. It helps teens understand the emotions and motives behind peer pressure and develop the confidence to make choices that align with their values. Role-playing different scenarios in which peer pressure might occur can be an effective way for teens to practice responding in ways that respect their own boundaries and those of others.

Preparing for Independence

As teens grow, so does their desire and need for independence. Emotional intelligence is key in preparing them for this shift. It equips them with the ability to make responsible decisions, solve problems effectively, and manage the responsibilities that come with greater freedom. For example, teens with high EI might recognize when they're taking on too much and decide to talk to their parents or teachers about adjusting their commitments. Learning to manage their own schedules, make choices about their activities, and deal responsibly with both successes and setbacks are all facets of independence that emotional intelligence supports.

Interactive Element: Goal-Setting Exercise

To further support the development of emotional intelligence during these transformative years, consider incorporating a goal-setting exercise. This can be a simple yet powerful tool to help teens articulate their aspirations and identify practical steps to achieve them. Here's how it works: have teens write down one personal goal and one academic or extracurricular goal. Then, ask them to list the steps they need to take to achieve these goals and how they will manage the emotions that arise during this process. This exercise fosters a sense of direction and purpose and enhances their planning and emotional management skills.

As we continue to explore the landscape of adolescence, remember that the development of emotional intelligence is not just about navigating the present challenges—it's about laying a foundation for future well-being and success. By focusing on these areas, you're helping to equip teens with the emotional skills they need to thrive as they step boldly into the next chapters of their lives.

8.2 Independence and Responsibility: The Role of Emotional Intelligence

When you think about stepping into new chapters of life, such as moving out for the first time, starting college, or entering the workforce, it's like standing at the edge of a diving board. It's thrilling and a bit daunting, but knowing how to dive—the technique, the timing, and the confidence—makes all the difference. Emotional intelligence (EI) serves as that diving technique in the vast pool of life's transitions. It equips young adults with the skills to make decisions thoughtfully, manage their emotions during significant changes, and maintain financial stability with a level head.

Decision Making and Emotional Intelligence

Decision-making is an art, and emotional intelligence paints its backdrop. EI influences decision-making by providing an awareness of one's emotions, the situation at hand, and the potential impact on others. This awareness allows for decisions that are not only logical but also empathetic and considerate of broader consequences. For example, imagine a young adult debating whether to accept a job offer in a new city. Emotional intelligence helps them weigh their excitement against their anxiety, consider how this move aligns with their career ambitions, and take into account how it affects their personal relationships. They learn to trust their intuition, recognize their feelings as valid data points, and use that information to make choices that align with their values and goals.

Managing Emotions During Transition

Transitions, whether moving to a new city or starting a new job, can stir up a mix of emotions from excitement to anxiety, anticipation to fear. Managing these emotions effectively is crucial for a smooth transition. Emotional intelligence teaches coping strategies such as mindfulness, which involves staying present and engaged rather than worrying about what the future holds. It also encourages developing a routine quickly in the new environment to provide a sense of stability and normalcy. Another effective strategy is emotional expression through writing, talking, or creative outlets, allowing emotions a safe space for release, reducing stress, and clearing the mind for better decision making.

Financial Emotional Intelligence

Now, let's talk money. Financial emotional intelligence might sound complex, but it's essentially about managing finances with maturity and foresight. It involves understanding the emotional aspects of money, like the desire for instant gratification or the stress related to debt, and handling them wisely. It's about making financial decisions that are driven by long-term goals rather than momentary desires. For instance, it's choosing to save for a significant investment like education or a home rather than splurging on immediate wants. This kind of intelligence includes budgeting, saving, and planning—skills that ensure financial stability and independence. Teaching young adults to set financial goals, track spending, and reflect on their financial decisions can foster a healthy financial life that supports their overall aspirations and well-being.

Building Support Systems

Lastly, no one is an island, and maintaining support systems is critical in nurturing emotional resilience and independence. Emotional intelligence involves recognizing when help is needed and having the courage to ask for it. It's about building and sustaining support networks, including family, friends, mentors, and professional help if necessary. These networks provide advice, emotional comfort, and practical assistance during challenging times. They also serve as a sounding board, helping to refine problem-solving skills and offering different perspectives.

Encouraging young adults to participate in community groups, professional associations, or online forums related to their interests can help them build these support networks. Additionally, maintaining regular contact with family and friends, scheduling regular check-ins, and being open about one's experiences and feelings can strengthen these support systems, making the journey through life's transitions smoother and more enjoyable.

As we navigate the complexities of independence and responsibility, understanding and utilizing emotional intelligence can transform potential stress into growth and learning opportunities. It equips young adults to face their current situations confidently and lay a robust foundation for future challenges and successes.

8.3 Navigating Romantic Relationships with Emotional Intelligence

In the blooming stages of young adulthood, romantic relationships often take center stage, presenting a new set of emotional landscapes to explore. Here, emotional intelligence (EI) becomes your guide, helping you navigate these relationships with awareness, empathy, and respect. Understanding emotional nuances enriches these connections and sets a foundation for healthy, enduring partnerships. Imagine this: two people holding hands, watching a sunset, not just sharing a moment but truly understanding and appreciating each other's feelings and expressions. This is the essence of emotional intelligence in romance—it enhances the connection by deepening the understanding.

The role of EI in romantic relationships is multifaceted. At its core, it involves recognizing one's own emotions and those of one's partner. This awareness can transform interactions, making them more thoughtful and nurturing. For instance, if you understand that your partner feels appreciated through words of affirmation, you may express your feelings and appreciation more verbally. Similarly, recognizing when your partner is stressed or upset—even when they haven't explicitly stated it—allows you to provide support in genuinely helpful ways, perhaps by giving them space, offering a listening ear, or engaging in an activity that you know helps them relax.

Communication and Conflict Resolution

Effective communication is the heartbeat of any romantic relationship, and emotional intelligence truly shines here. It encourages open, honest, and empathetic communication, ensuring that both partners feel heard and valued. Consider a scenario where one partner is disappointed by the other's forgetfulness about an important date. With high EI, the disappointed partner can express their feelings without blame, and the forgetful partner can listen empathetically and respond sincerely. This open communication fosters understanding and minimizes resentment, strengthening the relationship.

Conflict resolution, facilitated by EI, involves recognizing the emotional undercurrents of disputes and addressing them constructively. It's about understanding that conflicts aren't battles to be won but opportunities to understand each other better. Techniques like 'active listening,' where you really listen to understand rather than to respond, and 'I statements,' which allow expression without accusation, can be transformative. They turn potential arguments into discussions where both partners learn more about each other's needs and perspectives, facilitating a resolution that respects both parties' feelings.

Understanding and Expressing Love

Emotional intelligence enriches the expression of love by aligning it more closely with what feels meaningful and genuine to each partner. It's about understanding the different languages of love—be it words of affirmation, acts of service, receiving gifts, quality time, or physical touch—and knowing which of these your partner values most. For example, if your partner cherishes quality time above all, understanding this can guide you to prioritize activities you can enjoy together, thereby expressing your affection in a way that resonates deeply with them.

Moreover, EI helps in recognizing that expressions of love and affection can change depending on the emotional state or life stage of each partner. Being attuned to these shifts means you can adapt your expressions of love to meet the current emotional needs of your partner, ensuring that your relationship remains strong and flexible through life's inevitable changes.

Boundaries and Respect

A critical aspect of emotional intelligence in romantic relationships is understanding and respecting boundaries. This includes recognizing and honoring each other's emotional, physical, and time boundaries. Establishing healthy boundaries can prevent feelings of resentment or discomfort, which often arise from feeling overwhelmed or infringed upon. For example, if one partner needs some alone time to recharge, the other, with a well-developed EI, would understand, respect, and support this need.

Moreover, emotional intelligence involves communicating your boundaries clearly and respectfully to your partner, and being open to discussing and adjusting them as the relationship grows and evolves. This open dialogue ensures that both partners feel safe and respected, facilitating a relationship where both individuals can thrive.

In navigating romantic relationships, emotional intelligence acts not just as a mediator during conflicts or a guide in understanding your partner better; it's the very fabric that can hold the relationship together, making it resilient and adaptive to the challenges and changes life may bring. By fostering emotional intelligence, you enrich your relationships with deeper understanding, empathy, and respect, paving the way for a partnership that is not only loving but truly supportive and fulfilling.

8.4 Preparing for the Workplace: Emotional Intelligence Skills Employers Value

In today's rapidly evolving job market, the ability to navigate complex interpersonal dynamics with grace and understanding isn't just a nice-to-have—it's essential. As you or the young adults you guide step into the professional world, know that emotional intelligence (EI) is often the unsung hero behind career successes. It's the undercurrent that fosters effective teamwork, leadership, and resilience in the workplace. Emotional intelligence in the workplace goes beyond just getting along with colleagues; it involves understanding and managing your emotions and those of others to create a positive, productive work environment. This is why employers increasingly value EI skills when looking for potential hires. They know that employees who can manage their emotions, handle stress gracefully, and communicate effectively are invaluable assets.

One may wonder which EI skills employers are particularly keen on. Teamwork, empathy, and adaptability stand out as top competencies sought in nearly every industry. Teamwork is crucial because most professional settings require some degree of collaboration. An employee with high EI will likely be a team player who understands and manages group dynamics, contributes to and accepts feedback constructively, and inspires others to work together effectively. Empathy, too, plays a significant role, especially in leadership positions or roles that require client interaction. The ability to understand and share the feelings of another person can lead to better client relationships, more effective management, and a more harmonious workplace. Adaptability, the ability to adjust to new conditions, is particularly valued in today's fast-paced business environments. An emotionally intelligent employee can remain calm under pressure, adapt quickly to changing circumstances, and find solutions amid chaos.

Navigating workplace dynamics with emotional intelligence resembles balancing on a tightrope, requiring acute awareness of personal emotions and the intricate dance of office politics and colleague stress. At its core, active listening is a fundamental EI skill that fosters a deep understanding of co-workers' and supervisors' perspectives, enhancing mutual respect and minimizing conflicts. Similarly, emotional regulation is vital, enabling individuals to manage their feelings effectively, pausing to reflect rather than react impulsively to stress or critique. The pursuit of heightened emotional intelligence is an ongoing journey, mirroring the ever-changing landscape of work environments. It demands a dedication to continuous learning and feedback receptivity, crucial for both professional advancement and emotional intelligence development. Regular participation in EI workshops, discussions, and self-guided exploration through books or special interest groups is vital. Such engagements refine critical skills, setting the stage for career achievement and a significant impact on fostering a positive, efficient workplace culture.

As we look toward building careers that are successful, fulfilling, and conducive to personal growth, integrating emotional intelligence into our professional lives plays a pivotal role. It's about consciously understanding ourselves and others, managing our emotions intelligently, and approaching our professional interactions with empathy, flexibility, and a clear understanding of the shared human experience. These efforts ensure that as we progress through our careers, we excel in our roles and contribute to a healthier, more supportive, and more productive workplace environment.

8.5 Lifelong Emotional Intelligence: A Foundation for Success

Imagine emotional intelligence (EI) as a garden that grows and evolves over time, with the care and attention we give shaping its development and flourishing. It's a lifelong journey where the skills we nurture continue to expand and adapt through every season of life. This ongoing growth in emotional intelligence isn't just about enhancing our ability to manage day-to-day emotions; it shapes our personal development, enriches our life satisfaction, and prepares us to meet various life challenges with a resilient and open heart.

The Evolving Nature of Emotional Intelligence

The unique aspect of emotional intelligence (EI) is its limitless potential for growth, setting it apart from skills that may plateau. It expands and deepens as we venture through life's experiences, relationships, and transitions. This perpetual learning journey in emotional intelligence accompanies us from youth through adulthood to our senior years, offering new terrains of emotional landscapes at each stage. Whether navigating the complexities of parenting, career shifts, or the reflective process of aging, these experiences fertilize our growth, enhancing our self-awareness, empathy, and resilience. This continuous cultivation allows us to approach life's challenges with greater wisdom and adaptability.

Emotional Intelligence in Personal Growth

At its essence, emotional intelligence (EI) is integral to personal growth, shaping how we see ourselves and our interactions with others. A robust EI foundation fosters improved relationships, better mental health, and greater overall happiness. Self-awareness, a key component of EI, helps us recognize our desires and fears, leading us toward decisions that reflect our true selves. Empathy deepens our connections and broadens our worldviews, creating a sense of community. Furthermore, mastering emotional regulation, a fundamental aspect of EI, enables us to gracefully handle the ups and downs of life, enhancing our resilience and adaptability amidst challenges.

Challenges and Opportunities

As adults, navigating life's challenges requires a comprehensive emotional toolkit. Emotional intelligence (EI) serves as this toolkit, enabling us to manage family dynamics, adapt to new work roles, and gracefully accept the changes that come with aging. With EI, parenting becomes an exercise in empathy, allowing us to address our children's needs while managing our own emotions. In the workplace, it fosters adaptability and collaboration, transforming potential conflicts into opportunities for growth. As we age, EI guides us in embracing life's shifts, finding new joys, and maintaining an optimistic, engaged approach to life.

Strategies for Continuous EI Development

Continuously developing our emotional intelligence involves intentional practice and commitment. It's akin to tending a garden; regular care ensures growth and bloom. Self-reflection is a powerful tool in this developmental process. By regularly taking time to reflect on our experiences and emotions, we can gain deeper insights into our personal emotional patterns and triggers, which can inform our growth strategies. Mindfulness practices also play a crucial role, helping us stay connected to the present moment and manage our emotional responses more effectively. Engaging in lifelong learning—through reading, workshops, or therapy—can provide new techniques and theories that refine our understanding and application of EI.

Incorporating these practices into our daily routines isn't just about improving how we handle a difficult day or manage stress; it's about weaving emotional intelligence into the fabric of our lives, enriching every interaction and experience. As we continue to nurture our emotional skills, we not only enhance our own lives but also contribute to the well-being of our families, workplaces, and communities, spreading the profound benefits of emotional intelligence through every connection we make.

8.6 Mental Strength in Adversity: Tools for Tough Times

In every life, a little rain must fall, and sometimes, that rain feels more like a deluge. When you're caught in those storms, whether they're personal setbacks, professional hurdles, or unexpected crises, the strength to weather them doesn't just come from having a good umbrella; it comes from within. Developing resilience and leveraging emotional intelligence during these times enables you to navigate challenges with endurance, grace, and insight. Think of emotional intelligence as your internal weather system, forecasting, reacting to, and managing emotional climates, which can be particularly turbulent during tough times.

Resilience in the Face of Adversity

Building resilience is like strengthening muscles—the more you use and challenge them, the stronger they become. One effective strategy for developing resilience is through maintaining a mindset of growth and possibility. This involves seeing challenges as opportunities to learn and expand, rather than as insurmountable obstacles. For instance, if you're facing a particularly tough period at work, instead of feeling defeated by the stress, you might choose to focus on what this challenge teaches you about your limits, your resources, and your capabilities. Additionally, maintaining a routine that includes physical activity, adequate sleep, and nutritious eating can fortify your physical and mental health, providing a solid foundation for resilience.

Practicing mindfulness and meditation can also significantly bolster your mental strength. These practices help center your thoughts and emotions, reducing anxiety and increasing your capacity to manage stress. They create a space of calm in the storm, allowing you to view your situation with clarity and perspective. Engaging in regular mindfulness sessions—even just a few minutes a day—can transform your reaction to stress, helping you respond to challenges with a calm, focused mind.

Emotional Intelligence in Crisis Management

In times of crisis, whether in your personal life or professional arena, emotional intelligence is your best ally. It enables you to manage your own emotional responses and effectively navigate the emotions of others involved. For example, in a workplace crisis, such as a major project failure, using emotional intelligence can help you lead your team through the setback. By acknowledging the team's disappointment and stress, openly discussing what went wrong, and encouraging input on solutions, you foster an environment of collaboration and support, rather than blame and defensiveness.

Moreover, emotional intelligence involves recognizing when emotions might cloud judgment. It teaches you to take a step back, assess situations objectively, and make decisions based on rational thought coupled with emotional understanding. This balance is crucial in crises where high emotions can lead to hasty or harmful decisions.

Learning from Adversity

Every challenge carries a lesson, and the art of emotional intelligence helps you uncover and learn from these lessons. Adversity introduces you to your limits and capabilities, often revealing strengths you might not have known you had. It also teaches empathy by putting you in situations that you might not have understood otherwise. For instance, experiencing a significant professional failure might teach you about resilience and the importance of contingency planning, which can be invaluable in future endeavors.

Reflecting on these experiences and discussing them with mentors or peers can deepen the learning and growth that come from adversity. These conversations can provide new insights and strategies for handling similar situations in the future, turning past trials into future triumphs.

Support Systems and Resources

No man is an island, and during tough times, your support systems—friends, family, colleagues, professional counselors—become invaluable. Emotional intelligence involves knowing when and how to seek support and how to provide support to others. It teaches you to communicate your needs clearly and to offer help without overstepping, maintaining a balance of give and take that keeps relationships healthy and supportive.

Building and maintaining these support networks before you hit a crisis can make all the difference when challenges arise. Regularly engaging with your community, participating in support groups, and maintaining open communication lines with friends and family create a safety net that can catch you when you fall. Additionally, knowing about and accessing professional resources, such as counseling or therapy, can provide specialized support and tools for managing particularly difficult times.

As we wrap up this exploration into the tools for handling adversity with emotional intelligence, remember that the strength to face these challenges comes from a combination of personal resilience, strategic crisis management, learning from experiences, and leaning on your support networks. These elements work together to not only help you survive tough times but to emerge from them stronger and wiser. Now, let's turn our attention to the next chapter, where we'll explore how to apply these strategies in real-life scenarios, ensuring that you're fully equipped to turn life's challenges into opportunities for growth.

CHAPTER HIGHLIGHTS & ACTION POINTS:

- Emotional Intelligence for Teenagers: Preparing for the Transition

  - Adolescence involves significant emotional, social, and physical changes.

  - EI helps manage emotions, understand oneself, and navigate peer relationships.

  - Goal-setting enhances EI skills.

- Independence and Responsibility: The Role of Emotional Intelligence

  - EI aids in thoughtful decision-making and managing transitions.

  - Encourage mindfulness for stress management.

  - Educate on financial planning and goal-setting.

  - Support systems are crucial for resilience.

- Navigating Romantic Relationships with Emotional Intelligence

  - EI enhances understanding and empathy in relationships. Practice active listening and "I statements" in conflicts.

  - Effective communication and conflict resolution are key.

  - Understanding and expressing love meaningfully strengthens bonds. Learn and apply love languages.

- Respecting boundaries is crucial. Discuss and respect each other's boundaries.

- Preparing for the Workplace: Emotional Intelligence Skills Employers Value

  - EI is essential for teamwork, empathy, and adaptability.

  - Active listening and emotional regulation improve workplace dynamics. Develop active listening skills and practice emotional regulation techniques.

  - Continuous EI development is vital for career success. Participate in EI workshops and seek feedback.

- Lifelong Emotional Intelligence: A Foundation for Succes

  - EI grows with experiences and transitions. Make self-reflection a regular practice.

  - EI enhances personal growth, mental health, and life satisfaction.

- Mental Strength in Adversity: Tools for Tough Times

  - Resilience and EI help navigate setbacks and crises.

  - Building resilience involves a growth mindset and mindfulness.

  - EI balances emotional and rational responses in crises.

Now, to help you and your teen apply these concepts, let's break it down per area of focus. Start doing 2 action points at a time and work your way with your teen to apply all these.

- Navigating Adolescent Changes

  - Reflect on Emotions: Encourage teens to regularly

reflect on their emotions and discuss their feelings with trusted adults or peers.

- Stress Management: Teach stress management techniques such as time management, mindfulness, and open communication about school pressures.

- Identity and Self-Understanding

    - Self-Awareness Activities: Promote activities like journaling and self-reflection to help teens understand their emotions and strengths.

    - Positive Reinforcement: Provide positive feedback to boost teens' confidence and self-esteem.

- Peer Relationships and Peer Pressure

    - Role-Playing Scenarios: Use role-playing to practice responses to peer pressure and reinforce the importance of staying true to personal values.

    - Empathy Exercises: Encourage empathy-building activities to enhance social skills and understanding of others' emotions.

- Preparing for Independence

    - Decision-Making Skills: Guide teens in making responsible decisions by discussing potential outcomes and encouraging problem-solving.

    - Responsibility Management: Help teens manage responsibilities by creating schedules and setting realistic goals.

- Interactive Goal-Setting Exercise

    - Personal and Academic Goals: Have teens write down

personal and academic goals, listing steps to achieve them and strategies to manage emotions during the process.

By focusing on these, your teens can develop their emotional intelligence, helping them navigate adolescence with resilience and confidence, and laying a strong foundation for their future.

Conclusion

As we draw the curtains on this journey through "Raising Warriors," I want to take a moment to reflect on the steps we've walked together. From the early stages of decoding emotional intelligence in boys to preparing them for the complexities of the digital age and instilling resilience and grit for life's many challenges, our path has been rich with insights and strategies. We've explored not just the importance of nurturing emotional intelligence from an early age but also the critical need to develop mental strength and resilience in our boys.

One of the core strengths of our approach lies in the customizable emotional intelligence plans highlighted throughout this book. Each child is wonderfully unique, and these plans are designed to be tailored to meet your boy's specific emotional and developmental needs, thereby enhancing the personal journey you both undertake.

We also delved into the value of integrating interactive book components and addressing modern challenges. The interactive elements, online resources, and recommended games/apps we discussed are not just supplements; they are integral tools that enrich the learning experience, making the lessons more engaging and applicable. By tackling contemporary issues such as digital well-being and modern masculinity, we have ensured that the guidance remains relevant and practical in today's fast-evolving world.

Another key element we've explored is the value of building

supportive communities. The strategies we've discussed for engaging with schools, sports teams, or online forums are not just suggestions; they are invitations to join a network of support that extends beyond the walls of your home. This approach underscores the shared responsibility we all have in raising emotionally intelligent boys, reminding us that it truly takes a village.

Now, as you turn these pages into action, remember the profound impact you can have on your boy's emotional and mental development. I encourage you to implement these strategies and insights daily. Share your journey, the successes, and the challenges within your community and beyond. Your experiences can light the way for others, spreading the knowledge and support needed to raise the next generation of emotionally intelligent and mentally strong individuals.

I acknowledge fully that the path to raising emotionally intelligent boys is as challenging as it is rewarding. The effort requires patience, commitment, and a deep understanding, but the rewards—seeing your boy grow into a compassionate, resilient, and thoughtful individual—are immeasurable. Our ultimate goal is to prepare them not just for success in life but for a life characterized by emotional richness, resilience, and happiness.

I invite you to keep this conversation alive. Engage with your fellow coach, teacher, or dear friends who are also parents to seek continuous support and share these new ideas and challenges as you apply the principles we've discussed. The road may not be smooth, but I will cheer on you for even deciding to take action for your boy's sake.

Let's conclude with a note of empowerment and hope. Armed with the tools and knowledge from our shared experiences, you are incredibly well-equipped to make a significant difference in your boys' lives. Envision a future where these boys, raised with empathy, resilience, and understanding, lead their communities and fields, actively making the world a better place.

Thank you for trusting me to be a part of your journey in raising warriors. Together, let's continue to foster environments where our boys can thrive emotionally and mentally today and into the future.

Keeping the Game Alive

Now you have everything you need to help your boy succeed in life, one stage at a time, it's time to pass on your newfound knowledge and show other readers where they can find the same help.

Simply by leaving your honest opinion of this book on Amazon, you'll show other parents & caregivers where they can find the information they're looking for, and pass their passion for nurturing our young boys' emotional intelligence forward.

Thank you for your help. The importance of emotional intelligence on young minds is kept alive when we pass on our knowledge – and you're helping me to do just that.

References

- *Developmental Stages of Social Emotional Development in ...*
  https://www.ncbi.nlm.nih.gov/books/NBK534819/

- *Supporting the Development of Empathy*
  https://childcareta.acf.hhs.gov/infant-toddler-resource-gui
  de/infanttoddler-care-providers/emotional-development/
  developing-empathy

- *Create a Safe Space For Your Kids to Share Feelings*
  https://bridges2understanding.com/create-a-safe-space-f
  or-your-kids-to-share-feelings/

- *Parental Influences on Neural Mechanisms Underlying ...*
  https://www.ncbi.nlm.nih.gov/pmc/articles/PMC6756171/

- *19+ Innovative Ways to Teach Emotional Intelligence to Kids*
  https://positivepsychology.com/emotional-intelligence-fo
  r-kids/

- The Feelings Wheel: unlock the power of your emotions
  https://www.calm.com/blog/the-feelings-wheel

- *10 Role Playing Situations that Teach Compassion*
  https://meaningfulmama.com/day-339-compassion-role-p
  laying.html

- *Teaching Children Mindfulness can Help Them Regulate ...*
  https://www.fraser.org/resources/blog/teaching-children-

mindfulness-can-help-them-regulate-emotions-and-impro
ve-focus-

- *The impact of storytelling on building resilience in children*
  https://onlinelibrary.wiley.com/doi/full/10.1111/jpm.1300
  8

- *Growth Mindset is Crucial - And Not Just For Kids*
  https://possiblezone.org/blog/growth-mindset-is-crucial-
  and-not-just-for-kids/

- *Resilience guide for parents and teachers*
  https://www.apa.org/topics/resilience/guide-parents-teac
  hers

- *20 Examples of SMART Goals for Students and Fun Growth
  Mindset   Posters*
  https://www.atouchofclassteaching.com/20-examples-of-
  smart-goals-for-students-and-fun-growth-mindset-posters
  /

- *Top 30 Children's Books About Resilience*
  https://biglifejournal.com/blogs/blog/top-childrens-book
  s-resilience

- *9 Activities To Build Grit and Resilience in Children*
  https://biglifejournal.com/blogs/blog/activities-grit-resilie
  nce-children

- *Encouraging Emotional Intelligence in Boys*
  https://buildingboys.net/encouraging-emotional-intellige
  nce-in-boys/

- *Adolescent Mental Health in the Digital Age: Facts, Fears ...*
  https://www.ncbi.nlm.nih.gov/pmc/articles/PMC8221420/

- *A Case Study Looking at Social Emotional Gains in the ...*
  https://kimochis-media-marketing.s3.us-east-2.amazona

ws.com/FreeResources/Various/SEL-Case-Study-Early-Year
s.pdf

- *Screen time and children: How to guide your child - Mayo
  C   l   i   n   i   c*
  https://www.mayoclinic.org/healthy-lifestyle/childrens-he
  alth/in-depth/screen-time/art-20047952

- *How Your Child Can Improve Their Social Skills in Online ...*
  https://kinjo.com/blog/video-games-teach-life-skills-impr
  ove-social-skills/#:~:text=And%20even%20games%20play
  ed%20solo,teamwork%20to%20ethics%20and%20more.

- *Be Internet Awesome - A Program to Teach Kids Online Safety*
  https://beinternetawesome.withgoogle.com/en_us/

- *Male Role Models: A Complete Guide on Positive ...*
  https://mensgroup.com/male-role-models/

- *Addressing the Global Crisis of Child and Adolescent Mental
  .   .   .*
  https://policylab.chop.edu/article/addressing-global-crisis
  -child-and-adolescent-mental-health#:~:text=This%20met
  a%2Danalysis%20consisting%20of,COVID%2D19%20and
  %20subsequent%20lockdowns.

- *Teaching   Mindfulness   to   Children*
  https://newsroom.clevelandclinic.org/2024/01/17/teachin
  g-mindfulness-to-children

- *Resilience   guide   for   parents   and   teachers*
  https://www.apa.org/topics/resilience/guide-parents-teac
  hers

- *Developmental Stages of Social Emotional Development in ...*
  https://www.ncbi.nlm.nih.gov/books/NBK534819/

- *Yale   Center   for   Emotional   Intelligence   (YCEI)* https://medicine.yale.edu/childstudy/services/community -and-schools-programs/center-for-emotional-intelligence/

- *The Influence of Emotional Intelligence on Performance in ...* https://www.ncbi.nlm.nih.gov/pmc/articles/PMC6316207/

- *The Benefits of Teen Volunteerism: Transforming Lives and ...* https://www.nvfs.org/benefits-of-teen-volunteerism/#:~:te xt=Acts%20of%20philanthropy%20enhance%20self,under stand%20the%20world%20around%20them.

- *Building a Mental Health Support Network* https://www.embarkbh.com/blog/mental-health/how-can -i-build-a-support-network/

- *How to Strengthen Your Child's Emotional Intelligence* https://www.gottman.com/blog/strengthen-childs-emotio nal-intelligence/

- *Parenting children through puberty and adolescence* https://www.betterhealth.vic.gov.au/health/healthyliving/ Parenting-children-through-puberty

- *Peer Influence and Identity: A Parent's Guide* https://www.focusonthefamily.com/parenting/peer-relati onships-and-identity/

- *5 Life Skills Young Adults Need to Thrive - Newport Institute* https://www.newportinstitute.com/resources/empowerin g-young-adults/young-adult-life-skills/

Printed in Great Britain
by Amazon